I0805048

Voices of America

Edgecombe County

Edgecombe Remembers

Early dirt road work was performed by the county. (Courtesy of Edgecombe County Memorial Library [ECML].)

ON THE COVER

(background) This working tobacco farm was owned by H.L. Brake of Edgecombe County around 1930.

(foreground) Congressman L. H. Fountain and others inspect tobacco during an auction.

Voices of America

Edgecombe County

Edgecombe Remembers

Compiled by

Edgecombe County Genealogical Society

Edited by

Betty Reason, Traci Thompson, Minniejo Gay, and Dee Long

ARCADIA
PUBLISHING

Copyright © 2002 by Edgecombe County Genealogical Society
ISBN 978-0-7385-1432-1

Published by Arcadia Publishing
Charleston, South Carolina

Printed in the United States of America

Library of Congress Catalog Card Number: 2002104599

For all general information contact Arcadia Publishing at:
Telephone 843-853-2070
Fax 843-853-0044
E-Mail sales@arcadiapublishing.com
For customer service and orders:
Toll-Free 1-888-313-2665

Visit us on the Internet at www.arcadiapublishing.com

A farm gathering celebrates a successful harvest. (Courtesy of ECML.)

CONTENTS

ACKNOWLEDGMENTS

The Edgecombe County Genealogical Society would like to thank the Edgecombe County Memorial Library for their staff's assistance and support, as well as everyone who provided pictures, interviews, support, editing, or has otherwise participated in the making of this book.

DISCLAIMER

The oral histories presented here have been abridged due to space limitations. The full text and audio recordings of the interviews are available from the Edgecombe County Memorial Library and the Edgecombe County Genealogical Society.

Opinions expressed by the interviewees are not necessarily those of the Edgecombe County Memorial Library and the Edgecombe County Genealogical Society.

Introduction

History is the story of people—where and how they lived, their participation in community and national affairs, the types of entertainment and culture they enjoyed, and their connections with neighbors. History often records information about the famous—the politicians, the business leaders, those who capture the public eye. However, to really appreciate the lives of those who came before us, we need to learn about the lives of everyday people, not necessarily famous, yet significant for revealing the day-to-day lives of most people. An important way to gather such fascinating details is to collect oral histories, stories of folks told by themselves about their work, their homes, and their communities.

From the stories in this volume, we learn about life in Eastern North Carolina over the past 80 years. We find descriptions of life on the farm before and after World War II. We have accounts of mill workers and teachers, nurses and soldiers, all hardworking citizens who never saw themselves as anything special, just ordinary. Yet, their quaint stories are more than ordinary; they reflect the values of large families in church-going communities living off the land, of small-town life where neighbors know each other and help in times of crisis like natural disasters, the hard work ethic of farmers, and the patriotism of soldiers who leave their family to fight for freedom overseas.

Some of these stories may not be unique to Edgecombe County, but they are rich in details about life in rural Southern communities from the 1920s through the 1990s. These stories make us laugh, others make us cry, but all make us remember how it used to be, the good and the bad, the hard work and the fun, the life of everyday people—our neighbors, our friends, and our family.

Members of the Edgecombe County Genealogical Society (ECGS) have been collecting these oral histories for several years to preserve the history of the local citizens for future generations. The original purpose was to preserve the past, and there were neither plans nor funds to consider publishing these histories. The 15 stories in this collection are just a small part of the many stories that have been gathered over the years by dedicated individuals who have a strong desire to capture and remember the lives of people. Each interview represents hours of preparation, planning an interview (sometimes several), taping each session, and transcribing the tapes to be cataloged in the local library so that any one can come and learn about the people of this place. Much thanks to members MinnieJo Gay, Betty Reason, Traci Thompson, Dee Long, Frances Burgess, and many others who put this work together.

An earlier oral history project was organized by Maury York, former local history librarian, and sponsored by the Edgecombe County Memorial Library in the early 1980s. These stories focused on life during the depression on farms throughout the county. Several of those early histories are included in this volume. Both the work of Maury's volunteers and the work of the ECGS members are a treasure for all of us in Edgecombe to share. It is a priceless gift of memories. So, sit back and "listen" to the voices of Edgecombe County as they tell their tales.

—Monika S. Fleming

Ledger Clark Harrell of Macclesfield, North Carolina, enjoys his lifetime hobby of fox hunting. (Courtesy of Edgecombe County Memorial Library and Ledger Harrell.)

Chapter One
Farmers

Ledger Clark Harrell was born August 27, 1927. He is a unique, independent person who loves farming and fox hunting. Interview by L.G. Calhoun, June 10, 1987. Edited by Betty Reason.

Family Ties

I was born and reared around the Macclesfield area. My parents were Clayton and Annie Walston Harrell. They reared twelve children counting me. My brothers and sisters were Alice, Thad, Cad, Vonnie, Marvin, Gretchen, Clayton Jr., Helen, Gladys, Max, and Carson. I believe the oldest three was born in what's now Wilson County. The land has always been right on the county line, on what was my granddaddy's [Jessie Harrell] old place. And then my daddy bought a place and we moved down here to Macclesfield to make it more convenient for them going to school.

Then later he bought this farm here, and other property, back this way. Of course, he always farmed this land here since I can remember. He bought this land before I was born. I was born in 1927. Most of my brothers and sisters stayed until they got grown. The girls married, and most of them married to people that farmed. My six brothers, all of them stayed in farming most of their lives.

Ledger's Family

I married Virginia Anderson in 1948 and we have four living children and one that died when he was two years old. Two of my sons are still here helping me farm. The oldest one, Aubrey, has farmed all his life. He went and pulled two tours in Vietnam, two years in service and one year over there. He come back home and has been farming ever since.

Norris, he went to State College and graduated with a degree in agronomy. He worked around a little bit after he got out of college with a fertilizer company and a chemical company, but finally come back and decided he wanted to farm. All three of us, we just work together. They have their own crops but we just work it all as if it were one.

Susan, the only daughter I got, she works for the nursing home. I believe it is Beverly Health Care Center in Wilson.

Larry, I believe that he went to Wilson Tech for one year and then he got in patrol school. He's been a patrolman now for about eight to ten years.

Farming

We own some land and rent a whole lot more than we own. It takes right much for my two boys and myself. We farm all tobacco, that's what everybody is doing now. You have to tend so much more than you did a few years ago, to keep your head above water, or carry on the same standard of living that you have been used to. We raise a few hogs to help out.

Until tractors took over, all tobacco was trucked by mules. (Courtesy of ECML.)

When I was growing up, you used to tend the land with two mules. And the land had to be right close or somewhere not far down the road. People didn't travel to farm like they do now. You tended what you could with a mule and you had to drive a mule and wagon from one farm to the other. It had to be fairly close to do it. Now, you drive a tractor and leave it and somebody comes to pick you up. The tractor will go so much faster from one farm to the other. It is just so much easier tending than it was then.

Macclesfield has got the reputation of being one of the best tobacco areas in Edgecombe County. I think that is because way back there in the Depression when tobacco got so cheap people in this area hung on with it, stuck with it. A lot of the farms were small and it was more convenient for them to tend tobacco. It just got right down to where you had to have extra good tobacco, and they done that. They took up a lot of time with it and done it themselves. You might say they hand picked it and graded it and threw away all that won't just like they wanted, and came up with a grade of tobacco second to none. Of course, there's good land here, but there's good land all over the county.

There has been more soybeans planted around here probably in the last ten years than there's ever been. We used to plant right much cotton. I can remember when a lot of the people that farmed with my daddy planted cotton. But it just gradually got away from this part of the country. (Editor's note: In the 1990s cotton again became a major crop in Edgecombe County.)

I can remember us having some fodder and my older brothers would pull it. They would come up from plowing and have to go out and get it up before it rained. I never did help pull any, but I can remember helping them haul it up. They would go and get it and throw it under the shelter so it wouldn't get wet. As I got older they went to planting a lot of oats, cutting them with a mowing machine, and stacking them. Then later we got bailers and started bailing them so you could put them up in a much smaller place, but fodder was the main feed back there at one time.

First Tractors

The first tractor we ever had was a tractor Daddy and Mr. Tom Wiggins bought together. It had a disc and they thought that was the greatest thing that had ever been. That tractor could disc more land in a day than one man could with all them mules. It didn't have no horsepower and the disc wouldn't cut all that good. But it was great for them days! Then finally Daddy bought another one from Robert Lee Corbett. He was the tractor dealer, and Daddy got a free bottom plow to boot. From then on mules gradually got to be less valuable. Then people got to the one-row tractor in tending tobacco in this area. They thought that one of those tractors was all we'd ever need in this country. But gradually it went right on away to two-row; and now, the majority of people have gone to four-row.

Raising Tobacco

Fixing plant beds back then, everybody would try to get back in the woods far enough where they thought there weren't weed seed; you just had to clear up a place. Ever how many hundred yards you had to have; you'd just get out there in the woods and saw down the trees and grub up the stumps and start from scratch. In fact there was a lot of land that got cleared that way . . . on account of weeds and have to pick tobacco beds. You just didn't have time to pick them.

About the late '30's they began to use that Siami—I believe that's what it was called. That worked pretty good if you got some rain on it pretty quick. I think actually you were supposed to wet it but

Tobacco growing in the field (Courtesy of ECML.)

nobody had a way to wet it. So you just took a chance that it would rain and that worked fairly well. Then it wasn't many years before they come out with the plastic covers, which is what we still use. (This is just before the hot houses.) Now, you can just go out there and pick you out a good place and use it year after year.

Transplanting has been stepped up—now we are using two rows, compared to back then. You had to sit down there under the old-fashioned transplanter, right down there in the wheels, pulling all that dirt right back in your face. Now, you're sitting up there high enough where the dust don't bother you no ways as bad. Now, you just lay the plant in a forearm on the setter and it sets it out as it goes on down, everyone of them spaced the same distance apart. Then, if someone was off a click then there would be a close spaced plant and a wide spaced plant. The way we do the transplanting now is just a lot better and faster way.

Plowing has changed some, too. Now, you can plow two rows at the time and you have rolling cultivators, and compared to the old one-row plow with two mules, well, you can just plow so much more. Then, if a man plowed six or eight acres in a day, especially with a mule, he had done a big days work!

I can remember when we had to prime tobacco on our feet and put it in those old slide trucks, with mules pulling the truck. And maybe in a day's work you put in 400 sticks, or maybe 500 if you were lucky. That was a big day's work, and [you just] hung it up that day! That was a big days work!

They come along and got to leaving out the fifth row and you could go down there with a mule and with a dolly, they call it. That was the first step that came along to speed things up. They just made faster time. Then people got the looping machine, or sewing machine, and that was a lot faster than the old-fashioned way of looping. A lot of people were slow to go to them; it would cut the heads off and they didn't like it. There's always people who are right particular and they didn't like all those leaves falling out in the barn.

Then the bulk barns come along and that made all grades of change. Most of the people are now still using Long Harvester with four people priming the tobacco. I think you can actually get your tobacco more like you want it, than it does with a machine, because that machine is going to get

Long's self-propelled tobacco harvesters have made the work much easier. (Courtesy of ECML.)

A stick of cured tobacco is removed from the barn. This is referred to as "taking out tobacco" by most farmers. (Courtesy of ECML.)

the same amount when it comes along. If you've got people who know what tobacco to prime all through, you'll come out a little better off with the Long Harvester. A lot of times we will fill up two barns in a day. I don't know how many old-fashioned barns that would be.

Now, that Long Harvester, you ride it and prime the tobacco and send it up a conveyer and you have someone standing there laying the tobacco in the bulk basket. Then when they get the right amount on the rack, they just turn it around and send the empty rack on the back of the table and then put another rack on. The full one, they slide it into the trailer. Then when you get to the end of the row, just let that trailer down and you can hook it to a truck and that makes it convenient to move it from farm to farm. Because now you have all your curing facilities in one place.

This type of putting in tobacco usually takes eight on the harvester and we usually have one person hauling it and we'll have somebody at the barn to help him get it in the barn, so he can get back. If you have much distance to haul it, it takes time. We have about ten putting in tobacco in an average day, compared to the old way when we had three primers in the field, you'd have two loopers and four handers and the truck driver. That would be ten, but we only got four or five hundred sticks a day in an old conventional barn compared with two bulk barns with that same amount of help today. I expect that would be probably three or four of your conventional barn, now, I would think . . . just guessing.

One of the changes in tobacco harvesting is that the art of tobacco priming is gone. Back then you never had to tell a primer how many leaves to get, they just knew how many was ripe and that's what they got. They knew what they were doing. The average person now that you get, you just got to tell them how many leaves to get.

Another big change has been the use of MH-30, sucker control. That has been one of the greatest things there has ever been to help in harvesting tobacco. Back then the reason they couldn't tend no more tobacco than they could was the suckers. They would take the tobacco over if they won't broke out every week. Once they went to housing they just didn't have the time or the hands to keep everything done, and when the sucker got to growing it was just too bad. When they'd go to get the tips there would be so many suckers grown up through them you couldn't hardly find the tip leaves. The tip leaves would be sorry thin, and weren't no good. Now, you can put MH-30 on the tobacco and it'll hold them right down to September.

Swapping Labor

There is very little swapping labor done anymore. Everybody is set up now to handle his own. Back then, everybody worked together especially on the same farm. If there was two or three families, they would start housing tobacco and one family would put in on a certain day and everybody would come and help. Then the next family would put in on another day and everybody came to help them and so on. About everybody went to help them on their day except each family would leave one person home with the tobacco barn curing the tobacco.

Preparing Tobacco for Market

It's such a shame the hours that people have spent in a grading room when they could have been doing it the other way all the time. Day after day it took to get that tobacco in order and then sometimes it was dry and you had to re-order it by wrapping it up, to keep the same amount of moisture in it until you could get it sold. A lot of people had them ordering pits, great big pits dug in the ground, under where they tied the tobacco and they would put it in there to order. Some people would carry it back and put it back in the barns to order and some made their own rack to put it in. I have put a many of stick of tobacco, taking all I could tote, outside and dropped it right on the grass. We would do that late in the evening to let the dew fall on it. You had to get it up after it got dark, and pack it down and wrap it up. Then the next morning it would be softened up so it could be graded and tied for market.

Now, we just sheeted it right up. Back then, they had everything in grades—first, second, third, and fourth. Some of them would have as high as five grades out of one barn. They'd tie all day and then stick it up that night. They would pack it all together in a pile. They would notch the end of the stick for whatever grade it was. Then Daddy would send me around to pick it up to take it to market on that old truck. We usually carried two or three different farmers' tobacco at the same time.

When I'd get there they'd have it classed out; all the first grade in one pile, then they'd hand you that and you would put it up there. Then you'd put a stick to divide that and so on until all the grades were loaded. Now, when you go carry a load of tobacco, its untied and in a sheet. You just roll it right off into the truck, just like it come out of the barn most of the time. Of course, now you can stack it up and carry a whole lot more than you could back then.

A tobacco auction takes place on opening day. (Courtesy of ECML.)

Selling Tobacco

The first time I remember going to a tobacco market, Thad, my oldest brother, was working in Farmville. A lot of people in Macclesfield were selling tobacco there. In later years, I think my daddy sold most of it in Wilson.

I remember going to the market back during the war [WW II] and people were about to fight over the trucks. Everything was scarce including trucks, gas, and labor. It was always rushed around the warehouses during the war because the labor was scarce. When they were in there really unloading you could hear them tobacco grading sticks slapping on them cement floors, as they slid that tobacco off and into nice neat baskets.

I also remember that to ease the labor problem they brought in some German prisoners into the warehouses in Wilson to work. I saw some of the Germans in one of the warehouses. They were there helping get the tobacco off the floor. The first time I ever saw them I was about 16 years old and I took careful notice of them and their right white hair. That day they were putting the tobacco on the jacks so it would roll out to be loaded . . . and one of them stopped and punched the other and pointed at me. He was right blond-headed and he didn't look like he was much older than I was, but I guess he had been captured and sent over here. Ever who was with me that day told me, "He thinks you're German because you're blond-headed, too." I said, "Well, he's way wrong about that."

Recreation on the Farm

It wasn't all work; we had fun, too. We did a little fox hunting; we kept dogs that would run rabbits and bird dogs. Everybody in the family was hunters just about. Most of our hunting was done in the winter months. Then in the spring of the year, after we got up big enough, we played a lot of baseball, all over the eastern part of the county. We played ball around everywhere but the biggest thing we done was fox hunting. I remember when we used to hunt all up around Leggett. That was before there was deer in this county. We had big barbecues around somebody's farm and fox hunted a small round. That was a big thing back then, before deer hunting got so big. Of course, they still do a lot of fox hunting but it is a whole lot harder now than it was because you've got to break your dogs from running the deer before you can run a fox.

If my daddy was living on, I don't know where he would even try to fight the way it is now, just to hunt. His daddy [Jessie Harrell] was 65 when my daddy was born. His daddy had a pack of fox dogs and I've heard him tell about him and his daddy going hunting when he wasn't big as nothing. Daddy would ride an old gray horse and his daddy would ride an old gray mule. They would go over there around Fountain, down in there, and fox hunt. Then his daddy died. My daddy had a pack of fox hounds and kept on hunting. Then, when my daddy died, I had my fox hounds and I kept on hunting. I've got three boys and not a one of them care a thing about fox hunting, so when I get to old, why that'll probably be the end of fox hunting in the Harrell family. It's been in the Harrell family a long time, I would hate to see it go.

Back then they had corn shucking and tobacco tying. Yeah, I remember one corn shucking that my daddy had. We piled the corn up right over by the barn. I don't remember how much whiskey he got, but it sure got the men and young boys to come here and shuck corn. We went off rabbit hunting in the evening and they put me up a tree to punch an old rabbit out the hallow and I caught poison. When I woke up the next morning I was covered with poison and all swelled up. But we shucked that corn that night and everybody had the biggest time to be sure. That's the only corn shucking I remember but my daddy talked about them all his life.

The same thing with tobacco tying—it was going on a long time, as long as people tied tobacco. In fact, people had them clean up until they started to sheeting tobacco. Tobacco tying last longer in this community than the corn shucking did. Both of them were good to get people together and have a good time.

Macclesfield

I can remember when I was growing up, on Saturday night you couldn't hardly find a place to park a car all the way around that block down in Macclesfield. Now on Saturday, you won't even hardly find a car around there! The times have changed and people got better cars and better roads and they just go to more places.

I can remember when the town had tent shows. The merchants would go together and get somebody to come and show a movie once a week. It would be a free show for everybody here in town. Then later on in the fall of the year those tent shows would come around and stay a week. They showed mostly western movies and a little comedy. That played out when TV came along.

I guess TV's had a lot of effect on people around here. Now, people stay home and watch TV. I think it's had a big difference on children growing up. When I grew up there won't no such thing as TV. We played baseball in the yard; we were always playing games. Now my grandson, I bet he can't throw a ball across this room. Now, there's nothing but sitting in the house and watching TV every day. When young'ens get home from school, instead of getting out and playing they get them something to eat and watch TV. Of course time changes everything.

Future of Farming

I'm sure in the next 50 years there will be lots of changes in farming, though I can't see what it will be, but there is something coming along all the time. Just like curing tobacco; back then, people were putting tobacco in them old conventional barns and not hanging a stick but about so many inches apart, so the air could get through. If you had told them you could take tobacco and press it in a rack and slam it in a barn, they'd swear it would rot before the next morning. You couldn't have made them believe it! People are slow to change but not as slow as they used to be. There just ain't no telling what the changes will be.

The future of farming kind of depends on the young people. Farming is kind of like getting something in your blood. I think if you start with farming, it's something that you'll like and you grow into it and you'll continue on with it. In fact, like my two boys, they were raised up with farming and they both stayed with it. That's one reason I try to help them because I feel like if that's what they want to do and that is what makes them happy they should keep on farming. It gets to looking bad sometimes when we have a dry season or prices fall but it is just the way of life. It all may not be like we want it but I think that my boys are happy farming. They don't mind working and that's what it takes. Farming is a good way of life.

George R. Gammon is seen doing woodwork, one of his favorite hobbies. (Courtesy of ECML and Gammon family.)

George Roland Gammon Jr. was a farmer, a college graduate and service man. He was born on February 28, 1917, at Draughan and died February 12, 1994. George loved his family and farming. Transcribed by Pat Bass on May 19, 1987.

I was born on the 28th day of February of 1917. My early life was spent entirely on the farm. My schooling consisted of eleven grades then; before we finished high school we didn't have the twelve grades as we do now and I attended East Carolina Teachers College, for one year; and graduated from Oak Ridge Military Institute in 1937. From 1937 until 1942 I was active in farming with my father. In 1942, like about twelve million other American men and women, I was called into service. And I served from 1942 until 1945, a period of a little over three years. I spent many months overseas in Cairo, Egypt, and I was quite interested in Egyptian methods of farming.

Farming In Edgecombe County

Since then, '45, I got married and had been farming, and went to farming on my own in 1948. Farming has drastically changed since 1948. At that particular time we were using mules to farm. Mechanization had just begun. Most farmers would have maybe one tractor and a lot of mules. The most farming that I was doing at that particular time consisted of 30 mules I owned and rented property. At that particular time we had only one tractor and we knew nothing of cultivating, planting, and so forth, harvesting with tractors. Everything was done by hand labor. Every farm had a surplus of labor, and we were not industrialized and as a result people looked to farms for jobs and a lot of seasonal jobs.

In my early years we knew nothing about anything but mule farming. All was done by hand labor. Sometime, I think it was in the early '50s, I had the privilege of attending a seminar at Clemson University, and the economist that spoke, I can't remember his name, but the topic of his message was "Agriculture At the Turn of the Century," or "Agriculture in the Year of 2000." He would talk at length about what we could expect by the year 2000. He said we would see 100–150 horsepower tractors cultivating and planting six, eight rows at the time. We'd see no mules, in other words, mules would become a thing of the past. Our crops would be totally mechanized. Where we were using numbers of laborers we would use a minimum of laborers. Now this is 1987, and everything that he said has come true and we're still some 13 years from the turn of the century. It was hard for us to believe what he said could possibly happen. But it has happened! And I would wonder what would happen in the next few years.

Corn, back in those days, it was all hand pulled and you would shovel in the wagon and shovel out of the wagon. Anytime you wanted to shell any corn, you shucked it and you'd have a sheller on a box that would shell one ear at the time, very slowly. I can remember as a boy we were planting white corn. And in those day, to get our meal, we would carry our own corn to a mill that was located somewhere in our community; most every community had one. We would pick out the nice, big white ears of corn that was nice and pretty and we would shell those ears and be very careful with them. We had several cotton bags that my mother would keep laundered and we'd shell this corn, then carry it to the mill. The miller would grind it and he would take out so much, a certain percentage for toll, maybe 1/4th or 1/5th. And we'd bring the rest of the meal home and it was put in our meal barrel and these bags were washed. And they weren't used again until we went to the mill again.

A tenant farmer works in the field with mules. (Courtesy of ECML.)

In those early days everything was done by hand. Tobacco, we would have numbers of people prime tobacco on foot and truck it to the tobacco barn. And that was always a good job for us boys, to drive a tobacco truck. Kids loved to drive tobacco trucks. It was a good job that everybody envied. I think the reason was because kids six or seven years old had never been big enough to drive a mule or a horse and driving a tobacco truck was something they could do. That was quite a pleasure!

Tobacco was hung in these barns, and in the early days cured by wood. And somebody would have to stay with these barns night and day. I can remember neighbors getting together and having cooks at tobacco barns; maybe somebody would barbecue a pig. Maybe somebody would cook a Brunswick stew. That doesn't sound like it's a whole lot, but if you didn't have anything else to do that was a lot of fun. It usually took from five to seven days to cure the tobacco, and at the end of that time you would take it out, you'd pack it in the packhouse. Then you'd go through the same procedure again. Usually the tobacco-curing season would last six or seven weeks. Tobacco markets then would open well up into September. So, after you got through with this tobacco then you'd have to go back and grade and price this tobacco. When we would bottom this tobacco, somebody had to pull all these leaves off the stalk and put into our tobacco truck. Then people had to pick them up three or four at the time and hand them to another person, usually a woman that was looping them, and they would be tied on a stick. And that stick would be carried to the barn and passed up and hung on tier poles, and as I said, at the end of six to seven days they'd be taken out, put in the packhouse,

To maintain heat in the tobacco barn, the furnace must be stoked often. (Courtesy of ECML.)

Peanuts are stacked to dry in a field. (Courtesy of ECML.)

and when you got back to do it again, you'd have to take that same stick and take those three leaves off and carry them to somebody who was grading tobacco. And they'd have to handle them again grading. Again, somebody would be tying it; there would be a handful of leaves, tobacco leaves that were wrapped with another leaf, and it was then strung on a stick, packed down, and carried to the market. So, if you can think about how many times each leaf of tobacco was handled, you can tell what a labor-demanding crop it was.

Nowadays, all of that has been mechanized and you can see how many steps, how much labor that has been saved by doing that. Peanuts were planted with mules, one row at the time. They were cultivated many times; they were hand-chopped several times. And when they matured, there were poles set up in the fields. People would come along and stack these peanuts around the pole and they were dried by nature. Usually in six to seven weeks after they were stacked—they were usually stacked in September and maybe the middle of October or November—you could back with a traction machine which would take maybe fifteen men to crack the peanuts and bale the hay and all. And then they were put in bags and they were usually approximately 100 pounds. They were sewed up and again put in the packhouse and when you got through you would load those on your wagons or your trucks and you'd carry them to market and sell them in bags. Now, the human hand doesn't touch peanuts. In other words, they are planted and they are sprayed with weed killers and with insecticides. When they mature they are plowed up; then they are turned up to the sun for a few days. They are then combined and then they are artificially dried in these trailers. And when you unload a trailer you unload them at the market. So that saves, I'm going to say, 80 to 90 percent of the labor.

Cotton is another crop. We have heard of cotton pickers all our lives. In my early days it was not unusual to see fields with 50 or 60 people picking cotton. And these cotton sheets around the end of the rows and in the afternoons it would be weighed up. Each person's paid work would be kept separately and they were paid by the number of pounds that they picked. That was quite a job! Back breaking! Our other crops, too, have been mechanized. Another interesting thing that was done in those days was making our own molasses. Most farmers would grow maybe an acre of what we called sugar cane. And in the fall of the year it would be ripe for crushing and making molasses. What would happen, there would be some custom operator who would come around with a "crusher" and a "cooker." And the farmers would have cut the leaves off of these stalks of cane, which looked more like corn than anything else, and they would be cut and they'd bring it to a central location. Then these stalks were fed into a "roller" which a mule was pulling going around in a circle; and it crushed the juice or liquid out of these cane stalks. Right near by they had a big cooker, and it would cook for several hours. When it came out of the cooker it was then molasses. And most every farmer or farm family would have a barrel of molasses that would last them for the next year. That was always a fall activity, too.

Picking cotton the old way was a back-breaking job. (Courtesy of ECML.)

Race Relations In Edgecombe County

There are a lot of things about farming that I like to think about. One thing is our race relations. Back in the early days we had mostly black helpers, laborers on the farm. That was their only way then of probably making a living. And I would like to say that this period of change that I have mentioned, and that this gentlemen from Clemson was talking about, was propelled mainly by our black people. Maybe we should say "thanks" to them. It got to the place where industry had come in and they were able to get better paying jobs, which gave them better living conditions. Farmers were then forced into mechanization and it was a benefit to them and it was a benefit to us. Our farms this day and time could not afford as many people as were necessary to operate it in the '30s and early '40s. So, I'm going to say the black people have helped that a lot. Our relations with black people, I think, have been mighty good. Some of my best friends, now, are black people, people that have lived on the farm with me all of their lives. Their people lived with my people and their grandparents lived with my grandparents, so we've always had a good relation.

I noticed a question recently, "Why had the number of black farmers dropped so drastically?" I don't know what that was based on, but I would like to say that I don't know whether they have dropped any more drastically than other farmers or not. We've had fewer and fewer farmers every year, and what percentage I don't know, but I can't believe that the number of black farmers have dropped off percentage wise any more than the farmers in general. One farmer is doing what maybe seven or eight or ten did a few years ago.

A question that has been asked is "How has the relation between town and country people changed?" Well, when I was a boy coming up about the only time I went to town was to get a haircut. I remember very vividly a gentleman, incidentally it was a black gentleman who was running the barber shop, and he would come out in the country and cut our hair on the front porch, so we didn't have a chance then to go to town. Town people and country people are all the same now. We have a lot of people living in town that's farming. We have a whole lot of country people living in the country that are working in the town, and I can't see any changes, any difference in them in other words.

Life In Edgecombe County

In our early years a lot of people didn't have running water. I can remember at home, we had as far back as I can remember, we had running water but we didn't always have hot water. And we would have to keep that water for that bath, like you always heard about country people. But now your country homes and town homes are no different. Modern agriculture has come a long ways.

Where it can go to from now, I don't know. But, sometimes I think that maybe our knowledge and our "good learning," if that is a good expression, maybe sometimes hinders us rather than helps us. We over-produce, thereby making a surplus, and whenever we have a surplus the idea of doing something with the surplus comes in the factor of supply and demand. So, sometimes by producing large quantities maybe we are hurting ourselves rather than helping ourselves.

Another thing, today the farmers that have changed, those who have followed the times, are the ones that are doing better. And it seems to me, like sometimes maybe the younger the farmer, the easier it is for him to change. Maybe a lot of us old farmers were set in our ways and it hard-pressed us to change from the old traditional methods that were handed down. My father died in 1947 and if he could see what was happening in agriculture in this day and time he would never believe it. If I had been a Rip Van Winkle and had gone to sleep early in the '30s and wakened up now, it would have been hard for me to believe what was going on, too. Early in our farming years our farm people had no other way of making money. In other words, we weren't industrialized and people from the towns and cities would come to the farm looking for seasonal work, especially in the summertime and in the harvesting season in the fall. But now, people from the country are going to town simply because town has become very industrialized and offers employment for a lot of people.

An aerial view shows Long Manufacturing in Tarboro, a large manufacturer of agricultural machinery. (Courtesy of ECML.)

One of the early manufacturers in our county was Long Manufacturing Company. He was a pioneer in modernization of processing for curing tobacco and a major manufacturer of new agricultural equipment. He was a forerunner in combining and artificial drying of peanuts. He was a leader in bulk handling of tobacco. He employed a lot of people and we people in the country would always say that Long Manufacturing was doing more for the good of the area than any company we knew, because they were using mainly people in the country. And they were using these people; they'd take them and teach them. They were doing a good job and it meant a lot of income to the rural area.

When the Great Depression came along, I was very young. I can remember very well not having everything I wanted, but fortunately we never went hungry. We had what we needed. I'm the middle kid of three. I have a sister that's two years older and a sister that's two years younger. We were raised like most country kids were at that particular time. One thing I might say—and this will be hard for people to believe, some of them that are a whole lot younger than we are—women didn't go to see doctors when they were pregnant then. All of us were born at home. Our closest doctor lived at Leggett, which was then five miles from home. And we were born at home and apparently got along all right, and have done all right because we all three have been healthy all the time and we have raised families of our own.

I love to say that my mother and father were the best mother and father that have ever been and I'm sure a lot of other people would say the same thing about theirs. My mother and father had quite a good relation. I can remember my father saying that my mother was head of the house and he was head of everything out of the house. As the boy in the family, I was the one that would do more work in the fields and the girls were the ones that would stay at home and help my mother. We had a good life. As far back as I can remember we had running water at home. We didn't have the outside toilet like a lot of people I know of. I can remember very distinctly that my father made a frame out in the yard and had a barrel over it, and we use to fill the barrel up with water every morning when we were working. And the sun would shine on it during the day and we had a showerhead under the bottom and at night that's where we would take our shower; the water would be tempered by the sunrays. That was a good bath! We raised a lot of hogs when we were coming along and I can always remember having a smokehouse full of hams. My daddy traded hams to East Carolina College for the education of my older sister. That was during the Depression and I can see where things were mighty tight at that particular time.

We had electricity at home. We had our own Delco power plant. We'd have to start the motor in the afternoon and charge the batteries and we could have light. It was a lot better than lamp-light. When the motor would break down we could always see how lucky we were because we would have to go back and use the kerosene lamps. My mother cooked on a wood stove but we did have an oil stove. Most families did have oil stoves back in those days because using a wood stove in the summertime could sometimes be mighty hot. It was, but as soon as we were able to get electricity in the country, they went to an electric stove then. We did not have electric refrigeration; we had an icebox. Every town would have from one to two ice plants. It had trucks going through the country and they would deliver these three hundred pound blocks of ice maybe once a week. But in the early days when we were in town, usually on Saturdays, we would buy ice and bring it home and put it in this icebox. And that's what we used to preserve our food in.

We always had a big garden at home. My mother would can and dry food. You could dry apples. I can seem to taste those good applejacks right today that came from dried apples, which I don't see anymore. So, with a family like that, it's hard for the Depression to hurt a man; I think we got along mighty well.

Another thing I remember so much about as a young man is hog killings. Each family would try to raise and cure enough meat to last them the next year. And hog killing had to be done in cold weather. You couldn't have it any other time because we didn't have refrigeration. And, early in the morning we would get up and we would have a fire made around a big kettle, and call hogs; and neighbors from far and near would come to help quite a gathering at a hog killing. When they would come they would help with preparing the meat. I can remember cutting out the meat and grinding the sausage, and they would always have a pan and would cook some of the sausage to see that it was seasoned right. It seems like I have never eaten any sausage quite that good since. The meat was salted down and in a period of six or seven weeks it was washed and hung up in these smokehouses and it was smoked. Somehow they don't make meat like that anymore!

All farm families would have a big garden and I can remember the women getting together. They would brag, "I have canned a hundred and fifty quarts of tomatoes, so many quarts of peas, and so many quarts of beans." And it was always nice to see a pantry stocked with plenty of vegetables canned. We only had canned or dried stuff. It was a way of not having to go to the market. I wonder, today, if we would try living at home maybe our income would go farther.

Another thing I remember very much about my childhood is we went to Sunday school and church every Sunday. We never missed unless we were sick. I can't even remember my mother missing to cook dinner. She would either cook before we went or after we came back. I used to always say Saturday nights in the country were made for three things. One thing was taking a bath; another thing, reading the Sunday School lesson; and another thing was shining your shoes because we didn't have a whole lot of shoes. But we had to have them shined for Sunday school!

Farm Organizations

When I got out of service I was a veteran's instructor down at our local high school. There were programs that were geared to teach veterans and I was an instructor in that for three or four years. I have been a member of the Farm Bureau. I've helped with 4-H clubs. But my time was spent most with the draft board.

I was a director on the PCA which stands for Production Credit Association. That was a farmer-owned organization which farmers were able to borrow money for a short or intermediate term. Many farmers used that as a source of credit and a lot of money was lent in rural areas for that. The Production Credit is still going on, but like a lot of other programs, they have probably made some loans they shouldn't and they are having a lot of foreclosures and bankruptcies. So are the other lending organizations.

I was a member of the Edgecombe County Draft Board from 1948 to 1963. I have a certificate of appreciation from President Nixon for my 215 years of service. I'm a member of the Farm Bureau and I was executive director of the then Rocky Mount Production Credit Association in 1957. Then we merged with another association, and I served as a director from '57 to 1983. I retired from farming in 1980.

Borrowing has been the downfall of the farmers around here for a lot of reasons. Credit has essentially ruined everybody. Agriculture is so dependent on weather for just the right amount of rain: too much is too bad, too little is too bad. We have to make a bumper crop every year to payout. And if we have a year when we don't make bumper crops and we can't pay back what we have borrowed, it's hard for us to overcome it. And in one year it's almost impossible.

Maybe what we are going through now is going to be good because maybe the people who emerge and come out will be better managers. I do not know of many people who lost their farms. One or two have been in bankruptcy or foreclosure. I'm hoping maybe there will be a way that they will be able to redeem the farms. I never had a really bad year. I've had better years than others and I can remember one year that we had stacked our peanuts. We had a hurricane, and we stacked part of them and it got so wet that we were unable to ever get them out. I was planting then a little over a hundred acres of peanuts and we left a third of them in the ground that we never harvested, which was a big loss. But fortunately, our other crops that year did very well.

That was one thing about our farming here in Eastern North Carolina, especially in Edgecombe

County: we were diversified enough that if we had a failure in one, say peanuts, maybe our corn, tobacco, or cotton would take up for the slack. So, I think we were lucky by being as diversified as we were. I am the third generation to farm the land that I'm on, that I'm living on now, would belong to my grandfather. It was where my father and his people were raised. At his death he left me this farm and I've been living here since 1948 when I went into farming for myself. We have two sons, both of them college graduates, and both of them are in Raleigh, North Carolina. One of them is a French teacher and the other is an architect.

It is hard to get started in farming now. I can remember years ago and especially after the war when I was associated with the veteran's program, a young man could say, "Well, I'm going to farm for a few years until I can find something better." The capital outlay was not a whole lot at that particular time. For a few thousand dollars, they could buy them a tractor and get started and farm and make a living. But, with the price of machinery and the price of land, it is impossible for a young man to start out in farming and make a go of it unless he has some other form of income, maybe a rich uncle or maybe a father or a family member that will stake him. It's hard for me to see with interest rates where they are, with the amount of capital needed, with the amount of machinery required in this all-mechanized farming, how a young farmer can ever hope to pay for it. And the ones that we have this day and time are very dedicated. I know of some that got started earlier; they work long hours and I hope they are doing all right. They seem to be.

There are other jobs I know they'd rather do than this, and as I've said before a young man who comes to farm now must love farming; he must love to get out and feel the dirt under his feet and hear the birds sing and see the flowers bloom and see the crops grow because there are easier ways of making a living. I hope it will get better because too many of our people are leaving the farms.

Alberta Singletary Dail Best told a vivid story of life in eastern North Carolina. (Photo by Minniejo Gay.)

Chapter Two
Homemakers

Alberta Singletary Dail Best, the oldest of thirteen children, was born July 26, 1900 at Kinston, Lenoir County, North Carolina, and she died August 27, 1998 at Beverly Health Care, Tarboro, North Carolina. Her father, Benjamin Franklin Singletary, was born in 1878 and his wife, Lula Virginia Carlisle, was also born in LaGrange, Lenoir County, North Carolina in 1882 . Interview by MinnieJo Fisher Gay, August 5, 1997.

Life In The Rough

Our house was a shingle-top house; didn't have no underpinning and everything was woods. Oh Lord, I lived in the woods. The house had wood shingles on top and we didn't have no lights, a toilet, we sure did. Everybody did and we had a well with water we drawed up water at night and put in a bucket out on the porch at night to drink. Everybody drinked out of the same dipper. One of the dippers was a coconut hull and the other was a tin dipper and I reckon it cost ten cents, if we had ten cents to pay for it. That was our start off living—no lights, no running water, no indoor toilet.

At night the boys would come in from work and didn't want to wash their feet and they lay on that porch and slept and the goat got up there and slept with them part the time and part time went on off about his business. The hogs slept under the house and snored and the goat, too, and part of the time on the porch. Our cow would go off of a morning and stay all day and come back and we would milk her and she would go off again. Animals won't closed up, nothing was closed up. Didn't lock a door; slept on the porch, if we wanted to. No window shades and no window curtains.

It sounds like we were in a dump and we were. That is the way we come in this world and lived and everybody loved everybody. Everybody helped everybody and every year my daddy would grub up a streak of land and I didn't know whose land it was, but he got a whole acre of land to tend a small crop and he would sell some in the fall.

My mother, Lula Virginia Carlisle Singletary, was a seamstress and in the fall of the year my mother would take what money they made and she would go to town and would buy all our winter clothes, all we had to have all winter. That was when I was a little girl. She'd buy material for ten cents a yard and she'd buy near 'bout the whole bolt. She was a seamstress and she sewed for people wedding dresses and everything. She was talented. I had about three dresses and one of them was for nothing but church. One pair of Mary Jane shoes, black patent leather. I had a roll brim hat with a piece of ribbon on back of it and that was my Sunday hat and I went to church every Sunday. We didn't have clothes like other folks. We didn't have but two or three outfits. I think I had two dresses while I was going to school. When we came from school, we didn't wear our school clothes, we went and pulled them off and hung them up like they were worth a million dollars.

While I was gone to school she would wash the other one or she would make one and in the spring of the year she would do the same thing. By the time she done that, everything we had was rags. When the men's shirt-tails and drawers was wore out, then they would cut them up and make rags.

We didn't have no bought wash cloths, no towels, no sheets. She'd buy homespun— homespun is a loose woven cloth. She'd buy homespun and make sheets and pillow cases. It'd take about three days to get the homespun white. She put them in Lye water and wash them, get them all white. We didn't know what bought sheets was and when they wore out in the middle my mother would finish tearing them and sew the sides together to make them last longer.

Our clothes was washed on the wash board and two old wash pots. She would put them in there and boil 'em and I can remember right now how they smelled so clean, with box lye throwed in there with 'em.

She would make soap every year, enough to last another year. Most folks don't know nothing about that neither. Sometimes we'd have to bathe with that lye soap because the bought soap would give out. The soap he bought was that old long bar of soap, Octogan Soap, and he cut it in pieces to give us all.

Everybody had their own wash pan, an old tin wash pan, and everybody took care of their own. We'd would have a piece of soap and it was up to us to take care of it and know where it was at when we got ready for it.

We put wash tubs out and drew water up and fill the tub and set it to warm up in the sun so we could take a bath. We finally was able to buy a Majestic Cook Stove and you had a reservoir on the side, that you put water in, that heated up when you cooked the meals. It didn't supply enough warm water for everybody to have but we were fortunate to have that. It stayed hot all the time.

Well, we were happy! We didn't know no better and one time a year we'd get candy. He would buy a box of stick candy. He called us all in and give us a stick apiece. We didn't have no choice. He didn't let us have no choice for nothing. If we went to the table and she cooked five chickens and put on that table, we won't supposed to ask for no certain piece of chicken. They got up there and waited on us. We took what they give us. We got plenty and there won't no dispute or nothing. We'd fight sometimes but we's get over that.

Wash tubs were used for many jobs, such as washing clothes and making lye soap.

Christmas

When Christmas would come our mother would take the axe and take us and go into the woods—and it didn't make no difference whose woods—and cut down a little pine, or cedar, or Holly and we children would make things to go under it. We cut out doll babies out of paper and things like that and dressed it up and then she would get in there and cook cakes and take berries and trim the cakes up with them.

Christmas Eve you would see women come from everywhere all through the woods, wiping their mouths with their apron. I reckon they were dipping snuff. Come to see how your cakes were. Then go see how others cakes were, see which one had the prettiest cake. We didn't have nothing to give so it was just admire the pretty cakes and I tell you there was some pretty cakes cooked. They started cooking cookies about a month before Christmas. You can cook them and keep them a long time. We had a good life.

At Christmas time, maybe we'd get a present that cost a dollar, a little old mouse running up and down a string or something like that and we were as happy as we could be. The boys would get a fruit jar lid and nail it to a tobacco stick and roll it all day long chasing each another, having a good time.

We didn't go to the store and buy many groceries; we raised them—raised the hogs, cows, and everything we eat, just about, was raised on the land. We raised chickens all the time and sold them. My mother would get up in the morning and gather corn and cut it when it was in season. She would kill about four or five chickens. After I got older I would kill the chickens and turkeys, and didn't look at them either. Some of them got up and run away. She would get corn and stew it and cook about 50 biscuits and about pound of butter and put it on that table.

There were 13 of we children, a crowd of us, and there was a little country store down there that won't big as where we lived and Daddy'd buy our sugar and flour by the 50 pounds. The coffee we bought by 100 pounds, green coffee. This generation I don't never see none of that. But Papa bought it and they parched it and I had to grind it and smell of it and couldn't drink a bit of it. They would not allow children to drink coffee then.

We didn't hardly ever get sick and if we did get sick, Mother would go in the woods and dig up roots and herbs and cut bark off trees and boil it and use it and get us well. I know some of those old remedies now. If we had to buy medicine we'd buy Castor Oil, and Castoria, stuff like that, no expensive stuff.

They raised their own fruit. They didn't have to go to the store and buy it. After we done all that, parching that coffee, he would buy 50 pounds of cheese. I can remember cheese so good and I know we made cheese out of clabber and I eat my share of it. I loved cornbread and clabber.

Barn Raising

If they had a tobacco barn to put up and every man in that neighborhood was at that tobacco barn. A lot of times they were skinning the bark off logs with one of these long blades. They would build the sides and they had to raise it with ropes right there and did everything there was to do.

My daddy would have pea shellings, corn shuckins, tobacco tyings; they'd get together and sing, Lord have mercy, and parch peanuts and make pull candy. The men and women would square dance. Just good clean fun, I can't think of nothing they done wrong, they didn't hurt nobody, didn't kill nobody, everything was pleasant and everybody loved everybody.

The First Radio

Lord, have mercy, the first radio we got, unh! Everybody in the neighborhood thought, good gracious alive! Then everybody got to work, to get the other one one, and kept on until everybody in the neighborhood had a radio.

That gramophone with the big horns. The tapes are round. I believe that thing is in the neighborhood of Lenoir County now. If I was able and could, I would investigate because my daddy wrote down everyone of those tapes in the lid of that box.

We sold that thing, after he died. We got so disgusted, there was somebody there all the time wanting to play it and my mother sold it to Betty Murphey and I would not be surprised if it ain't somewhere in her family. She's dead and gone. That was the way we had of getting good music. You have to wind this one once in a while.

About one night a week, my daddy would have the neighbors at his house. He had the only gramophone and everybody in the neighborhood loved it and they all got together and played music. We children would lay on the porch on the floor and the men and women would take the chairs. We didn't have enough for everybody. The chairs were made by Granddaddy. Grandmother had a whole set. Her whole furniture was homemade.

My grandmother, Betsy Cobb, knitted most of the socks that the men wore. She pieced up bed quilts. We had fun with her. She was nearly 90 years old when she died. She was the nicest, cleanest old lady you ever saw but she was the ugliest, hateful acting somebody as could be. There's folks like that now. When my grandmother died, we didn't have funeral homes and the doctor had to ride in a buggy and was driving with one of those old plow lines. You didn't know when he would get there 'cause it took so long to get there. But when she died we didn't have no way to go anywhere but in a two-horse wagon or a one-horse wagon or cart.

Undertaking the Old Way

They laid grandmother out that day when she died. People began to come through the woods everywhere. Everybody walked. Some shrouded her to put her away and that night they sat up with her. Everybody sat up with the dead. They kept camphor rags all over her face all night. Camphor keeps the dead from foaming at the mouth. The funeral homes do away with all that.

My daddy always had a big packhouse out there, place to build and that people could go to. The men folks would gather what planks and timber they had and you would see them coming with timber on their shoulder and they would get in there and make a coffin, won't no caskets along then. My mother helped pad and line them—the women folks got together, not only my mother—and they were made with pink in them, not made like they are now.

That afternoon when they come to get her body, we were getting arranged to go and here they come out with the coffin on their shoulders, four men, and put her in there and then took a big screw driver and screwed it down. That was for good, it wouldn't be opened no more.

They had this hearse thing that was open with a frieze around the top but I don't know where it come from. There was two men drove it with two horses. They put we children all in a two-horse wagon. That's the way we went to funerals, behind the corpse. They got us all in that wagon and I had on my Sunday outfit. There was about two one-horse wagons behind us and we went out and got on the road to the cemetery. It won't but about four miles but felt like a hundred on that wagon.

We got up the hill and my hat flew off! You could've heard me holler a mile! I screamed so hard. Well, the men that was going to bury her was right behind our wagon and the wagon wheel run over my hat! One of these men jumped out and got that hat and put back on my head and got it straightened out and I was worse off than the woman that was dead. Cause I was upset as worse as you've ever seen anybody. I just messed up things sure enough and I won't but about six years old. I've always laughed about that.

We got back home and the folks in the neighborhood come and brought some food, what they had. At night you would see lanterns all in the woods where they were coming to see you. It was dark and there were no lights no where.

Yes we had lanterns, too. Can you imagine what that was like? I didn't enjoy washing oil lamp chimneys. Had to wash chimneys that smoked up every day. We burned kerosene and I don't know of no other oil that was burned at our house until we moved up near Hugo and he got a farm. Hardly made enough to pay the bill. We got gas lights. We were lucky to get some in our house and we felt like rich folks, having lights. I quit washing lampshades. From then on we got one old light bulb sticking down in the top of the house and you pulled a string and that made a light.

Walked about a mile to school when I was a tiny thing. I never rode to school and I never carried a lunch basket because I stayed close enough to walk. I didn't ever do ugly about that but one time. One of the girls out there had some biscuits punched with a hole and molasses in it. I thought it was nice to go to school and carry your lunch and I didn't have the privilege of doing that. So that day she asked me to stay with her and eat and I did . . . but my daddy beat me near about to death when I got home because I was supposed to show up at home. Now along then, you got your whippings but it didn't murder you up or nothing, but you knew where they stood. It made a different person out of me. I would stand on the back porch and when they rung that bell at school I would fly across that cotton patch and get in line at the tail end.

I went to a one-room school for a long time. The teacher boarded with us. My music teacher did too. So you had to have something a little decent. I went to Hugo School. There is a nice little church there now but the school has been torn down. It is between Kinston and Hookerton. That was my hangout place in Grifton. What little hang out I did was on Saturday evening when I might get to go to town.

The school house was on one side of me and church was on the other and when we'd sweep yards we'd sweep both yards. No grass growed in nobody's yard. Didn't none grow in ours. If any grass growed, my daddy'd say get a hoe or you pull it out. Then we'd take these old dogwood limbs and make yard brooms and go out there and sweep the yards.

We had ducks and Mama'd pick them about once a year. That was a job. Honey, everybody in the house had a bed. Everybody slept on feather beds. When they'd get wet, we'd throw them out on the fence and let them dry and put them back on the bedstead.

I got my back-end beat with a violin, I sure did. Daddy played the violin his self, had a snake tail in it. I mean they cut the rattlers off and put them in there and it done something to that violin, and it made pretty music. One day I talked ugly to my mama.

When we went to school in the morning we had our bed to make up and we'd go out the back door to school. And that morning, the colored girl come to clean up and do the washing and I had made the bed. I knew I had and mama called me back and said "Bert, you come back here and make this bed up." I said, "I made the bed up." Then she said, "Well, it's not made up". What they did, they went in there and pulled the sheets all off it and curled the quilts up and left them curled up. "I said, "I know durn well I did." Honey, my daddy was settin' in the window, playing the violin and when I said that, I didn't go to school in a long time, because he beat my back-end raw and whipped me with that violin. Sometimes, I wished he had busted it. If we said anything ugly he would got on our butt and he won't long about it.

Jingle, Jangle, Jingle

One day I was out there at the two-horse wagon. They kept that two-horse wagon just like you do your car. They washed it and kept the wheels clean and shining because that was all we had to go on and I did love that two-horse wagon. I was settin' on the tongue, you know they hook the chains in the tongues and they would jingle and make music. I loved to play music with no music, and I was just settin' there on the tongue of that wagon, having the best time playing with it and it was so soothing and nobody bothered me. I won't rearing and tearing up something, the chains were hitting together and making a jingling noise and he come up and saw me. Honey, I ain't never touched a wagon no more, playing with it. It made him so mad he could have killed me but we knew not to do things like that but there won't no harm in it. I could'a broke the tongue of the wagon.

I was just riding the old Jackass up there in the lot one day. I had a horse, but my horse was so humble, she won't fittin' to ride, that's the truth. But that mule was dangerous and there won't nobody home and I got up there and rode that mule, held onto his ears and rode that mule with nothing holding on but me. That scared daddy, because he had told us not to go about that mule. The mule would kick everything around him, you know how they done. I rode that mule all over that lot three or four times and didn't get hurt. Now you know the Lord was working with me. My daddy whipped me that time. He whipped me more times than a little; my mama never whipped me to amount to nothing. She would just take it and go on. I got mad that time over the bed, because I did make it but they made me make it again and whipped me to boot. I put on a pair of his drawers before he got in there. When I knew I was going to get whipped I'd put on a pair of his long drawers and he didn't know it. I sound like he was mean, but he was a good daddy and he took care of things around where he was at and everybody knew it.

Drunk as a Coot

One of the best memories I have as a child is on that bicycle on that trail. There'd be five or six of we girls and we didn't have nothing but old bicycles and our dad liked to worked himself to death to get us that. We would wear our hats backward and we took an axe and cut out a trail. It was all woods. The boys cut too. So we would have a place to ride. We'd get out there and sing and climb trees. One time we got drunk as a coot out there. We climbed, people don't mess with pine trees no more, but long then pine trees were a plaything. You could get one and swing all day long and wouldn't break it. It would look like it would be broke but it won't. Old Miss Callie Harris had a little store down there and she was an old maid. So one day we were out there in the woods back of my house. One of the boys or girls suggested going to that store and we would take eggs out of the nest and go down there and shop. Maybe an egg would buy us a piece of candy or something. The boys went down there and got a little bitty jar of snuff in a can and a half plug of tobacco. They came back up there and got in the tree and we dipped and spit on each other. We were the nastiest things you ever seen. We spit all over each other and the boys they spit and then got sick, fell out and puked

Yard brooms were used for discipline as well as sweeping!

all over everything. My mama didn't know what was the matter. She thought I had got hold of some liquor somewhere and they had a time that day. All us children was sick and nobody wouldn't tell how. They could see how, but didn't know how we got it, cause we didn't have no money. But we had some eggs. It was just a comedy the way we lived.

That's the kind of mess we lived in but honey it was a happy life. I was proud of it. Then we children began to get grown. I was the first one married, I was the oldest and then on and on.

The First Telephone

I was 15 years old before I got a telephone [in 1915]. I was spending the night in Ayden, with the preacher and his wife, and when my daddy called me and told me I had a telephone, honey, that man had to carry me home that night. I liked to had a fit over that telephone, course I got plenty a slaps over it. I'd get on it and wouldn't get off it and papa would spank me in the face sometimes. But I enjoyed that telephone. From then on we got able and bought a little farm, lived on it, and raised a little crop until we got better and better, but we have had hard times.

First Car in the Neighborhood

The first car that was in the neighborhood belonged to Joe Smith, and when he'd crank it up everybody in the whole neighborhood for a mile would get to that road so they could see that car. It was an old Ford and went clacker, clacker, clacker, all over everywhere. And we children just had fun with it but we didn't see it but once a week. They didn't take it out everyday like you all do.

Courting Days of Miss Singletary

Courting days started when I was in the choir at church at Hugo and played the piano at that time. I did not care anything in the world about music. My daddy did everything in the world he could and the music teacher did too. I loved other folks' music but I didn't want it. I was in the choir that Sunday and played the piano and Leo Dail saw me and said he knew immediately that this was the woman he was going to marry. He come out there with Lawrence and stood there looking at me and told the man, "I'm going to marry that woman." So after service, he come up with Lawrence and he made me acquainted with Leo and we went together until we got married.

He had a horse and buggy, rubber tired, sun top, and that ain't all, a robe to put over your lap, a switch to pop the horse to make him dic, dic, dic, dic. That courting stuff was something in this world.

Swamp Fire

One night we went through a swamp there going to church and that swamp fire got under the wheels. The fire would come right up on the wheel. And Lord, have mercy, I jumped out of the buggy, right over the wheel. Scared me so bad. Leo said, "I swear, I thought you'd gone crazy." We went to church one night and went to get out of the buggy. He helped me out and don't say folks didn't wear short skirts and tight skirts. They did! I had a skirt, up to my knee, my mother wouldn't let me wear it now, I don't reckon. He let me get out of the buggy. When I hit the ground, I said "Did you see my activity?" Just kidding him, you know! He said, "Yeah, I saw the damn thing and didn't know what it was." He ain't seen nothing and that was some expression for young folks to make, won't it?

A whole crowd would go on a wagon to church at night, not only my family but every family.

I Joined Church

We were going to church at Hugo but I won't far from home. We had revival at that church and I joined church at 15 years old. I thought I was the best Christian in the world. I told them at church recently that if I had died that day I would'a went straight to Hell, because I was not saved. I went that way about 12 months or longer and there was about 15 of us and they got the crowd together and we were baptized.

I didn't know nothing about a creek. I hadn't seen no water no wider than a house but we went to a little creek. Somebody had cleaned up all down both sides so pretty. We didn't have any blankets, what we had were quilts, that we made. So we got our quilts and got in the one-horse wagon and went down to that creek. It seems like it took a month to get there, but it didn't take long. Now-a-days, they got a place to take a bath and dry off and go back to church. But we didn't have nothing but the woods, and so we went on down there and lined up to be baptized. When we got there they tied the old mule and we got out and lined up and went on down to the river. There were some women had on long aprons tied in the back and bonnets on and the men had old black floppy hats on. They were singing, "Shall We Gather At The River." I can hear it right now. Got down there and bless my Lord, I was the first one to go in and I looked at my preacher, Reverend Harris. I said, "I don't want to do this." He said, "Well now, you have pledged and you are going to have it to do," and so we did. Got it over with, washed off, and went back to that wagon and wrapped up in that quilt and had to ride all the way back home wet because we did not have any where to change. I can hear those folks singing right now some of the sweetest songs on that river, sweet singing in this world. Well, I thought I was saved, I thought I was the best girl in the world. Kept going to church and it went on and on, and I was married and had one child before I was really saved. Before I realized what it took to save you and it was worth it. I said I hope there is not a one in here who is as dumb a Christian as I was, cause I was not saved. I was baptized. So I told it that night at that church and that is when the undertaker heard. That man was saved that night. And the next Sunday they said his little boy was saved.

At The Beach

It's like living in two worlds. What did I know about a beach, nothing! I don't care if I didn't! When we went to the beach I would get up in the morning sometimes and make jellyrolls. We had to work

In the 1920s young people liked to travel by boat to get to the beach

hard for what we got. I would cook jellyrolls and pack them in a box and we would go down to the beach and that was something. Sit around on the sand and eat jellyrolls, didn't even have money to buy drinks with. Young folks has everything they ask for today and don't have enough.

Long then it would take one day to wash and one day for my mother to iron and another day to scrub and now we wash and do all the housework in one day. Had to fix three meals a day, went to the orchard picked up the fruit, went to the garden, dug this little thing and that little thing, cooked it, and by then it had gone late.

We didn't know no better. Our activity was riding through the woods on the bicycles. You could hear them girls come a whistling and, I reckon, if you'd see that now it'd be a disgrace. There would be 15 or 20 of us. Boys and girls didn't get together neither. The boys went one way and the girls went another. But you'd better believe they would protect that sister though. It was a different way of living.

Lipstick and Jewelry

Our make-up was red tissue paper. We would buy red tissue paper and wet it and make our lips red. I reckon we looked like Indians with that on there but everybody used it, some used pink tissue paper. It was pretty to me, I'll tell you that. We didn't go for jewelry. We made our own out of berries. We'd go in the woods and get chinaberries and cook them and skin them and dye them and make beads. We dyed them with paper.

I looked like an Indian, fat, plump. My face was broad. People used to ask me if I was kin to the Indians. I didn't know it was such a thing as an Indian. I had a lot of hair, wore it plaited all the time, just like an Indian. I took it down the eve before I was married and I never put it up after.

Because I was the oldest, the smaller children in the family would always get information from me that won't worth five cents.

The Flu Epidemic of 1918

My daddy died when he was 40 years old and he died in 1918 in the flu epidemic. The day my daddy died there were two tenants women on the farm that died and if daddy had known it, it would have broke his heart more. They told him they were not dead, but they were. Those two women were hard workers on that farm, they plowed and done anything. Janie Tilghman and a colored woman, I don't remember her name, but they were hard workers. Honey, Daddy was a Mason and there won't enough Masons hardly able to bury him.

I didn't go because I won't able. I was home with pneumonia and I had had my baby. Everybody was sick; I had two brothers who went to the hospital that same evening but they pulled out of it. My husband's mother took my baby boy and carried it to her house, and they wrapped me up in a bed quilt and put me in the back of an old Ford and carried me up to her house and I stayed there until I got better.

World War II

Pearl Harbor was in 1941 and one of my sons was shot at Pearl Harbor. I reckon he had that bullet when he died. He went through all of it and then got back home and had brain cancer and died. I lost two boys. Uncle Sam got my baby boy. He won't but 22 years old in World War II. He was in about two months when he got killed in Germany by snipers in 1942.

Married Life

Leo Dail was raised in Edgecombe County. We were living in the country on a farm. Farm life doesn't change much. You can say what you please about this old stuff. I used lard in collards and things we cooked. That's why mine's better than anybody else's. We killed hogs and put the lard in the stands and sometimes now I think about it, there'd be about 200 pounds of lard setting in our house at the same time and it didn't rust. We did use stone but we finally got some tin lard stands and then we put sausage in the stands and heat our lard in the pot and pour it over that sausage, and, honey, we had sausage all the year. We canned some too; spare ribs and things like that.

Farm folks back then didn't put poison on our Irish Potatoes and collards. We went out there and picked the bugs off and the worms off the tobacco and killed them.

I didn't go out on a public job, I stayed at home. That's the pretty thing about women in my day when I was growing up; the women didn't go out and work like men, they stayed at home and raised children. In this day and time it shows on the children, you know it does. My children never give me no trouble. I've always wanted to be partners with my children as best I could.

We had three daughters, Virginia, Selma and Barbara. We lived on the Jenkins Farm on the Speed and Oak City Road, the Scotland Neck highway. We lived near Mayo's Cross Road and my best friends lived there. My husband died there May 4, 1973. I run a florist for a while and I retired from that. That was about the biggest thing I did.

My mother died at 69 years of age in Farmville, North Carolina. She married again and had another child and now that child is dead. All of us is about gone now. Out of the 13 people, I've got two sisters, Naomi Rougemore of Lakeland, Georgia, and Bet Singletary Dorian of Grifton and brothers Ben and Dan Singletary

I married next Albert P. Best who had children by a previous marriage; Mary Best Little of Greenville, North Carolina; Edna Best Howell of Fayetteville, North Carolina; Lewis and Norman Best of Tarboro, North Carolina. Albert was born May 29, 1893, and he died in August 1986—almost 93 years old. We built this house here in Tarboro.

I've been through a whole lot and the children have, too. There have been things we wanted and needed and didn't have, but that's all right.

Bessie Duke came to Edgecombe County with her family when she was five years of age (Photo by Minniejo Gay.)

Ms. Bessie Duke was born in 1906, the daughter of Walter Duke (1876–1945) and Mollie Powell (1873–1944). She had three siblings, Edward Duke (1898–1944), Matthew Duke (1900–1935), and Clarence Duke (1902–?). She lives at her home in Whitakers and still works in her yard, tending her flowers. Interview by MinnieJo Gay, December 3, 1998.

School and Play

I first went to school down at Worrell's cross road in Edgecombe and then over at the Bloomer Hill Center where we now have all sorts of meetings. My first teacher was Sofie Dawson. The school was located where Speights Chapel Road crosses Highway 33, out of Whitakers. There is an apartment on that corner now. Mr. Raymond Worrell and Mrs. Violet Worrell used to run Worrell's Store across from it on the other corner. Sandy Taylor's son Pat Taylor has a feed mill down Speights Chapel Road, and the school I attended was not too far from there on the opposite side of the road.

We didn't have no kind of stuff to play with except we did have one of those gramophones a long time ago that played the round records. It had a big horn. We children living down here on Cutchin Street did all the things we were told to do and just played with each other. Ethel Battle [Duke] and Alfred Davis, across there where the path is, had sons Brisco and Charlie; they're dead now. Clarence Davis is living in Rocky Mount in a rest home. His wife was Mamie Powell, my cousin. When we played, I called Clarence my son and we played and we were real close. Mamie had a son William Thomas Lindbergh Powell and he was called "Boot Jack."

My best friend when I was a child was Beatrice Arrington. She would spend the night with me and I would spend the night with her. I loved her and she loved me. I was living here; she was up in the country. We would go fishing three or four days and carry dinner and water. Went to Beach Ridge and the Marl bed and catch red fin, perches, eels, and catfish. Now you can't fish anywhere; all the land is posted.

Life on the Farm

When I was a child living on the farm, we raised chickens and hogs, and after mother died in 1935, I still raised chickens and hogs myself. I have carried eggs to town and sold them to Mr. Herbert Etheridge at his store. When I killed the chickens I would cut off the head with an axe and I would shoot the hog in the forehead with a rifle. I loved making sausage and I made good sausage and used chitterlings and stuffed the sausage in them. A farmer down the road, Mr. Jimmy Nunnery, and I used to work in hog killing. They used the bought casings and gave me all the chitterlings. You clean them and rinse them and turn them inside out and soak them all night in salt. We used the chitterlings and stuffed the sausage in them the old way and hung the sausage to dry.

Right after we killed hogs we trimmed all the fat off the backbone, around the hams and shoulders, and cut it up and put it in the washpot. We put a little water in the pot to get it going and then cooked it and stirred it to keep it from sticking. In later years we put a teaspoon of soda in there

These hogs were killed at the Fisher farm in 1947. (Photo by Minniejo Gay.)

when we took it up to keep it from getting rancid. This would be stored in stands and we used it all year.

When we first killed the pigs and cut them up, we packed them in salt and let them stay about a month to cure and then take them out and wash them. Then we would put the molasses and black pepper on them and hang them up and smoke them. That's the way I done mine. The weather had to be cold to keep it from spoiling. You used most of the freshes.

Hurricane Hazel came through. We were grading tobacco in the fall of 1954 in the packhouse, my sister-in-law Eula Duke and me. My sister-in-law Lizzie Dickens Duke lived across the street and the wind blowed her gate open. She went out there to shut the gate and fell and broke her leg. I was looking right at her from the pack house window. It blowed something in this house. I think it was the roof off the kitchen and dining room. It blew chimneys over, you could see things blowing, like awnings flying, barns twisting. That was the first time we knew about a hurricane. Then Hurricane Donna came. Always call them women's names and they say it's 'cause they are so mean and change directions!

Neighbors

This house was built in 1911. I lived in that house on the corner across the road, this side of that new church. We moved from that house to this house. The land was bought from the Watsons.

Mr. Owen Gay, an older man, lived on down the road and his brother, Mr. Norman Sr. overseered on the next Braswell Farm. They had a brother, Dick Gay, lived down on the other Cutchin place and he

Bessie Duke's home is in Whitakers, North Carolina. (Photo by Minniejo Gay.)

used to come around and sell the best watermelons. I used to work in tobacco with Mr. Norman Gay and we used to call that place "Caledonia." Worked five days of the week at $3.00 a day. Mr. Norman Junior Gay talks about working for 50¢ a day when he was a junior in high school and I used to chop cotton for 40¢ and pick cotton for 25¢ a hundred pounds. That won't nothing! But when you think about it, we could buy a cola for a nickel and go to the show and eat a hotdog and drink for 50¢ or less.

When Mr. Junior was growing up his daddy was the overseer for Mr. Henry Braswell and he said he used to haul wood for Uncle Dave, a black tenant on the farm. He and Aunt Dink Fountain stayed there on the farm, too. They were brother and sister. He'd hauled a wagon load of wood for 10¢ a load for Uncle Dave and one day Uncle Dave would not pay him and he told him he was going to take it right back to the woods. Another time Uncle Dave told him about somebody stealing his chicken and he heard the chicken holler and he ran out of the house in his night-shirt and chased the thief. Uncle Dave said the chicken kept calling him, "Caaack Cack". "I'm coming, I'm coming!" Uncle Dave said, and he got so close that the thief dropped his hen! The stories he told were like Uncle Remus stories, and he had a long grey beard, too.

Mr. Fletcher Coker owned his farm up there on the left beyond Mr. Owen Gay—Mr. Fletcher and Maude Coker. That little house is still standing that they lived in. Mrs. Coker would go to town walking. You know she never learned to drive. Their granddaughter, Brenda Wadsworth, lives there and has a pretty house back in the woods.

Others have lived around here as long as I have. Cora Hunter was Arthur Hunter's wife and she is in her 80s and Colleen Debrew, Colleen's sons worked at American Enka—Spencer and Leon Debrew. Colleen lived in the old Otis and Vick Parker Weaver house, the two-story house beside J.M. Cutchin's Mule Stables. Colleen used to walk every day as long as she could and she is in bed now. I miss seeing her now. She used to go to church and sing in the choir and I miss seeing her. I still go to church, and I go to different churches when I get a way to go. Willie Fountain lives right out there next door. Eula, was his wife, he called her "Mouse." He still lives in the same house with his granddaughter. His horn sounds like a rooster on his car.

William Watson and his wife was Rena Watson that are buried here on this road, they lived in the big house near the corner in the middle of the block. He was a school teacher. They must have growed up here. Charlie and William and they were here when I first knowed them. It was there by the Watson Cemetery that I called myself seeing a ghost. My cousin Clarence Davis and I were always fooling one another. I was coming down the road by myself, coming from the show or somewhere. I thought I saw my cousin but it looked like the Watson man. He vanished. I know one time here, and my daddy won't dead then, and we were coming from my neighbors house and I thought I saw my daddy in the yard and then he went away and I thought he went in the house and found out later he had been at the tobacco barn stoking the wood furnace curing tobacco like they did with wood instead of oil burners. You had to keep the fire going.

Arthur Battle and Dave Battle are buried out there near the Watson graves. Dave Battle had a barber shop and Carter worked on the farm; he didn't have no kind of business. They had a sister named Pearl Battle and Annie Maude was Dave Battle's wife. On the street about where the water tank is, Dave Battle had Battle's Pressing Club and Barber Shop, and Grady Nelson had The Shoe Shop and Barber Shop.

Whitakers

Most of our shopping was done in Whitakers. I remember when the streets of Whitakers were crowded, especially on Saturday. We bought from Mr. Latham, at that same location where Bradley's Store was, canned goods, groceries, and stuff like that. He had two little pigs in the store feeding them two kinds of feed to see which one grew faster. They could do anything then. I used to do washing for that family. Miss Mary Latham was first grade teacher at Whitakers School and died May 1998 in Tarboro. I did ironing for them.

Latham's Store later became Bradley's Store. (Photo by Minniejo Gay.)

Whitakers had the outdoor toilets near the water tank. That was about 20 years ago. [There is] a house across there which still has a toilet out back. I burned mine up, glad to get rid of it.

Those mule stables that Mr. Mack Cutchin built are still there, about to be taken over by cars. I seem to remember Tom Burnette worked there. When mules would come in on the train, Tom would take a horse down to the depot and the horse would lead the mules to that stable. Mules will follow a horse. They did not have to load them on a truck from the Depot.

The loggers really mess it up when they get logs out of the woods. They say this road out here went behind the house on the Braswell Farm. You used to be able to see the bed of the old road but loggers tore up the woods when they last logged in there, but I remember the road where it is now. Mrs. Lena Cutchin Bradley said that it used to be a stagecoach road that went behind that house and the back of the house was really the front of the house.

I do remember the Hearne coffin factory down on the railroad here in Whitakers. And the first policeman I remember in Whitakers was Mr. Bob Weaver and he had a son, Robert Weaver. Then when Mr. Denby was policeman, a train hit a car and knocked the engine of the car across the street to the door where the Whitakers Oil Company was. It was Reginald Etheridge's Dime Store.

FAMILY

Jerusalem Church was purchased about 1905 and is located behind the church, which is on Cutchin Street Extension. It was there when I grew up and a cemetery was over behind it in the field. Mr. William Foreman Carlisle, a civil engineer, owned the farm when that cemetery was started and he rented the farm to Walter and Octavia Bryant Etheridge. He took meals with the Etheridges and lived in a house in the yard. There was a colored man, who dropped from a passing train, and lived with Mr. Will. He kept the cemetery clean. I can't tell you who all buried there, there are so many folks: my granddaddy, James "Jim" Powell; and grandmother, Susan Rosley Powell; and my daddy, Walter Duke; and mama, Mollie Powell Duke; two of my brothers, Matthew and Edward Duke; my youngest brother, Clarence Duke, died and was buried in Richmond; cousin, Mamie Powell Davis; Aunt Henrietta Powell Battle; and a lot of peoples are buried out there.

My son William Earl Duke was born April 3, 1935. He made some liquor one time and they caught him and they came by and told me to come out there. I said, "I ain't coming out there cause I ain't made no liquor." I never did go out there. It seems like you could buy, I reckon it was boot-leg, most anywhere in town. I could hear people talking about that sort of thing. My brother and daddy had trouble with alcohol, but I never knew Daddy to go to the doctor in his life. My brother came up here drunk and my son, Walter, saw him and he said " I ain't never going to drink no whiskey" and he never has drinked. He retired from Barko Lounger with 32 years of service. He does not like it when you say folks need to get out of the lounger and into the rocking chair. He said, "Now you are talking about my livelihood." My son fixed the lawn mower so I can't start it. He keeps the grass mowed for me.

I enjoyed talking about life like it was. This present generation will be able to at least read about it. I would like to tell them to be nice to everybody, nice to old folks, to be good and kind to everybody.

The county sheriff breaks up a whiskey still. (Courtesy of ECML.)

Beadie Webb, David Webb, and grandson David stand in front of Handy Corner Grocery. (Courtesy of Helen Webb.)

Beadie Webb was born August 21, 1907, and died March 7, 2000. She was a Nursing Attendant and a generous, charitable, and independent woman. Interview by Betty Reason, 1992.

Early Years

I was born in Wilson County, over there on Grandma Sally's [Sally Harrell Webb] place, where Reddick [Reddick Webb] lived. And I was born at home. Mama [Quilla Webb] did not have a doctor as far I know. My mama was about 26 when I was born and she was 18 years old when she got married. We moved from there when I was one month old down here to Macclesfield in 1907.

I was named for my father's mother. My full name was Levinia but in the Bible its listed just Beadie Webb. I had one sister and four brothers. I was the fourth child.

Dow Webb was the uncle of Beadie Webb; Beadie spent a lot of time with him growing up. (Courtesy of Helen Webb.)

My daddy [Barney Webb] worked as a hired hand with my grandmother [and] her husband; my grandfather Riddick was dead. When we moved to Macclesfield, he ran a barroom. I never remember going inside the barroom but they told me someone would come to the house and get me to lead Uncle Dow home. Uncle Dow would get "too much" and he would follow me anywhere and I would take him by the hand and he would follow me home. I imagine I went in that respect but I was too young to remember. I wasn't but five years old when my father died.

I just do remember definitely when my daddy died. I remember he slept on a cotton pillow because he had asthma, emphysema, or something like that . . . . He came home from the barroom one day and lay down on the porch and told me to go get his pillow. I knew which one because his was the only cotton pillow in the house. I went and got it and he never went back to the barroom again. He died in about two weeks, in July of 1912.

Mama and Aunt Demie sewed and they made our clothes. Boy's shirts were made. I don't know about their pants, but their underwear and all that kind of stuff was made. Dresses, slips, and panties were made. We wore shoes, then they were called shoes. We call everything we wear on our feet shoes now, but back then we didn't. There were slippers and shoes. Shoes had high tops and we wore them in winter time. Some were buttoned and some were lace; we had some of both kinds. We also had Bear Brand stockings, and most of them were black. We also had what we call homespun stockings—thick, brown stockings. Women had silk stockings but they were just worn on Sunday. After that they were taken off and put away to the next Sunday.

I don't remember being treated any different from my brothers because I was a girl. I imagine them being older, there was some difference. My two older brothers were always in to something. I remember they tied two cat's tails together and hung them on the clothes line to see them fight and if they didn't get a whipping! Mama whipped them boys good fashion. But my two older brothers had to work real hard because my Daddy died when my older brother was 12 years old. The other one was ten. Mama farmed after Daddy died, with the help of Uncle Dow and Uncle Willie. There was Veneable, Curtis, and Mama to work; Chaney was older than I was. She was seven and I was five; John Dawson was three and Barney Battle was on the way when my Daddy died.

I did most anything that came along on the farm except priming tobacco and breaking up ground. You see Veneable and Curtis, with Uncle Dow's help, did all that and they did it with a one horse plow. They had no cultivators. If you had a cultivator you were a high-fluting farmer.

We farmed across the swamp from Macclesfield on Mr. Jim Pitt's place. We walked over there to do all that farming. We tended some up there near Ledger Harrells too and lived right here in Macclesfield. We lived right here on the corner, Mama did, and Aunt Demie lived here. She had no children and she helped look after us and I kind of took up with Aunt Demie. That is why I have this house right now. They [Demie and Dow Webb] moved down here in 1902. They bought it from Mr. Jim Forbes who was living in it. He was going to build him another house so they bought this one from him.

I just do remember going to Tarboro on, they called it the Yellowhammer (East Carolina Railroad). I remember going there with Aunt Demie. I got to go places with Aunt Demie. I went more than Chaney did because Mama was bogged down with the children.

I started school and finished school at Macclesfield. I made two grades in one year. You see Aunt Demie took so much time with me, I was sort of ahead. Not that I was bright—she had taught me a lot. I graduated there at Macclesfield High School in 1924. What a wonderful day that was! I thought I was grown, had all the education I'd ever need and I would never need nothing else. That's all I knew! People in my class were Ruth Batts, Mary Bridgers, Alfonsa Felton, Bea Bridgers, Turner Griffin, Bea Lewis; Mary Webb and Nellie Owens were two of my teachers. Mr. Crawford was principal and he did some teaching after I was in high school. Other teachers were Mr. Stevenson, Nanny Batts, Miss Dixon, and Miss Saunders who turn out to be Mrs. Robert Lee Corbett. Mrs. Reneford taught me and Mr. Reneford taught us once when we made such a flunk out in a book called Agriculture.

We cut up so bad over that book that he had to come in there and teach us. We were just having a good time, we thought we knew as much about farming as they did. We thought we knew it all about farming, and there was nothing they could teach us.

Back then nobody courted until they were about 16 years old. They might have courted a little bit before that age but not much. But I guess every little girl and boy had someone they thought was special. I remember Wiley P. Harris was mine. I thought that he was the prettiest thing. They had a box party one night and Aunt Demie had fixed me a box and Mr. Pete Harris [Wiley's father] thought that that was wonderful, because I had a box. He let Wiley P. buy it. Oh! I thought that was wonderful. We were just little bitty things. I remember, he was buried down there about where the Barbecue House is. They moved the cemetery when they started the Macclesfield Cemetery.

As far as dating in high school, we weren't allowed to date during the week, just on Saturdays and Sundays. During the week, you came home got your clothes changed and you worked until supper time, you eat, and then you did your studies. Work and schoolwork came first. Mama saw that we went to school. I finished, Chaney finished, but the boys, Mama couldn't do much with them after they got a certain age. They would outdo her. She would send them, but they would skip and not go. Curtis quit in the ninth grade. He had the sense in the family even after quitting. He sort of educated hisself later.

Aunt Demie told me if I wanted to go to college, I could go. Mary Bridgers, a good friend was going and she thought I might want to go, too, but I didn't much want to go and leave home. I've wished I had of gone. My life would have been much different.

I accepted Christ down here at the Christian Church when I was a teenager. Aunt Demie saw that I went to Sunday school, but she didn't push me to go to church. After I got up some size I started going to church.

I never remember my Mama voting, but I knew Aunt Demie to vote. I remember one time she and Uncle Dow had the biggest fuss, because Uncle Dow was going to make her vote the way he wanted her to vote. She said, " I wouldn't vote that way to save your soul." And she was the only one to vote the Republican ticket down here in Macclesfield that year. She voted the Republican ticket to show him he won't going to boss her.

I don't remember much about Prohibition, because I wasn't into it, but I do remember they would sort of slip it in. I remember one time I broke a whole gallon that was brought in for Christmas. I picked it up to see what it was and dropped it. I knew what it was I guess, but he had brought it in and I just wanted to see what was in the bag. I didn't get a whipping over it though.

Later Years

When I got married I lived in Wilson County. When Mama moved back over there I was about 14 years old. I was still living here in Macclesfield with Aunt Demie. My grandma told my Mama if she wanted to move back over there that she would give her everything she could make with a crop and she might get along much better. But in about a year Mama wanted me to go home, because she said Chaney and I would never know each other as sisters if we didn't live together. I remember so well Aunt Demie telling me this was my home and I could come back anytime Mama would let me. Well I got up there and got hooked up with that young crowd and I didn't want to come back to Macclesfield.

I was 17 when I got married and David was 24. He was David Webb, the son of Joe and Mattie Webb. He was just one of the Webbtown group; I don't even know the first time I met him. He was part of the group, and I just took a liking to him and him to me. We didn't have no big wedding. We were married in Wilson by the justice of the peace, in a little office, in 1924.

I never worked away from the farm until David died. We moved to Macclesfield about four years before he died. We moved back the fall of 1965, and he died in March of 1968 of a stroke and rare heart disease. We had three children, two boys and a girl, Helen, Brooks, and Ronald Dow. After he

Pearl Webb Jones, David Webb, and Beadie enjoy a winter day. (Courtesy of Helen Webb.)

died I took a little nursing course and worked at the Nursing Home. But that was after my children were grown and away from home.

Depression

I would say that the Depression had the most impact on my life, because along then people just didn't have the money to buy things, you just couldn't get it. We didn't suffer. I'm not saying we didn't have enough to eat, because we did. You had to be so tight with your money to make sure you had enough to survive on. You just did what you could to get along. We had a big garden, a potato patch; we canned, raised our own meat, had our chickens and eggs and all that. We had plenty to eat but little else. Nothing was left for anything extra. We had to buy sugar, flour, and meal, that was

Demie Harrell Webb was known as "Aunt Demie" to many in the Macclesfield area. (Courtesy of Helen Webb.)

the main things we bought. Washing powder, Gold Dust, was the first washing powder I ever saw. We didn't get much of that. I might get a box every once in a while. We had box lye soap. We made our own soap.

ELECTRICITY

When I was growing up there was no such thing as electricity. We didn't know what it was. We had old kerosene lamps and Mama had an old pedal sewing machine. Everything was done by manual labor. You carried in wood to burn in the wood stove and the same for fireplaces. We didn't have no heaters. I didn't get electricity until after all my children were born, sometime after the depression. Though they had it in a lot of places, we didn't get it in the country until sometime in the 1940s. I didn't get an electric washing mashing until 1949 or '50s, an old wringer type. It was wonderful just to have that! I had an old ice box before we got our first refrigerator. We got a second-handed one first and it kept enough fuss to keep anybody in the world awake all night long, but it made ice and we really thought we had something.

FAMILY THINGS

The only family things I have are from Aunt Demie not my Mama. Aunt Demie was my Mama in a sense; she didn't give birth to me but she took me under her wing and it was like I was hers. I have a quilt, two pictures of children, and a frame from the barroom. Seems like the pictures came from selling salve. If you sold enough salve you got a picture. (editor's note: These are beautiful old oak frames with pictures of busts of little curly headed boys and girls.) The frame on the mirror, there were two of those that came out of the barroom. One, Aunt Demie had and Mama had the other.

ANCESTOR STORIES

I don't remember it but I was told that my granddaddy left home for about two to three years, and my grandma Beady took him back just like he never left. They said John, that was my granddaddy's name, never said where he went. She stayed home and farmed with those boys, my daddy, Uncle Dow, and Bert. They must have had land, and they kept things together until he came back. But Grandpa John did go to the Civil War, but this was after the war. I guess he just wanted to wander some more. They told me she took him back as if he had just walk out the door for a spell, and it was never mentioned between them again. They said she was a good person. They said she raised Old Man Ruffin Hyman. All the colored people around here were leaving and going to another state, I don't know for what. They come by to get Ruffin to go. They said she told Ruffin that he was free to go if he wanted to go, but he didn't have to because as long as she had a home he would have one, too. He didn't leave; he stayed on with her until he was grown.

HOLIDAYS

After I was married, nobody around had Christmas trees and I remember being the first in my neighborhood to have a Christmas tree. But Aunt Demie always had a little one for me and I continued it with my children. When they were about 11 or 12 we started to having a big tree. Aunt Demie had given me all her decorations from over the years and I would add to it. It was nothing fancy but it was pretty to us. It didn't even have electric lights. We kept Old Christmas, Aunt Demie, Mama, and I did, too. We didn't do anything much different, except that absolutely no work was done on Old Christmas.

Well that is my memories, I hope they mean something to somebody in the future.

William Brown and Eva Mae Johnson were the parents of Mary Alice Johnson. (Courtesy of Mary Alice Johnson Mills.)

Mary Alice Johnson, a devoted mother and grandmother, has lived in Edgecombe County all her life. She enjoys sewing, crocheting, and cooking. Interview by Pamela Edmondson, 2001.

CHILDHOOD

I was born on February 23, 1932, in a house located about two miles outside of Tarboro to an unwed 16-year-old mother, Eva Mae Johnson, and William Henry Brown. My mother had three children: me and my brother, Elbert Jack Johnson, born July 1, 1936. Between us was a brother named Carter Pope Jonson, who died of diphtheria when I was very young. I do not remember him in any way; however, later in life I saw a picture of me standing at his grave. I do not remember the incident. After my brother and I grew up and left home, my mother and step-father, Walter Dew, adopted a child named James Edward Dew. He is younger than both of my children so he seems more like my child than my brother. My mother was a twin, born January 26, 1916, The twin named Mae Alice died in June 1916. She had an older sister named Annie Bell and older brother named Joe Jack Johnson. My uncle Joe died of lung cancer and a few years later my Aunt Annie died of Alzheimer disease. My mother died September 1990 of lung cancer.

When I was six years old, I started first grade at Central School, which was the school at the end of the Commons. It was between Panola and St. Patrick Streets. It had been renamed Bridgers School before it was torn down. I left that school and went to Tarboro High School on Johnston Street. Sixth, seventh, and eighth grades were upstairs in the building and ninth, tenth, eleventh, and twelfth grades were downstairs in the same building. I graduated in June 1950. The old Tarboro High was located where the Martin Middle School building is now. The only part of the school left there now from when I went to school is the auditorium. While spending time with my Aunt Annie, I went to church at St. Anne's Chapel, located on the corner of Howard Avenue and McNair Road. The old church is still there, but the stained glass windows have been removed. While growing up on the farm, Mama and Papa would bring us to town on Saturdays to go to the movies. There were two theaters then—the Majestic near the present day Simmon's Furniture store and the Colonial in the building across from the post office. We would see a movie in one theater, walk down the street, and see another movie in the other one. During my later years I would go to the dance on Friday nights at the Leggett School, which is now North Edgecombe High School. Later they started dances in Tarboro at the old Hart Mill Recreation Hall. They had dances there on Saturday nights and on Sunday morning. Trinity Baptist Church held church services in the same building.

One of my earliest memories was the day my grandfather, Jack Johnson, died. He and my grandmother were arguing. He had a sore knee and was using chloroform liniment to rub on it. While they were arguing, he got mad at her and swallowed some of the liniment. Bill Bardin, who was Sheriff Bardin's son, and another man came to the house and carried him to the old Edgecombe General Hospital which was about two blocks away. They pumped out his stomach; however, it was not successful and he died. It was listed as a suicide by drinking chloroform. The next death in the immediate family was my grandmother, Julia Wallace Johnson, when I was 14 years old. She lived

Julia Wallace Johnson poses on Highway 250 at the service station. (Courtesy of Mary Alice Johnson Mills.)

Walter Dew and Mary Alice Johnson are photographed at the Foxhall farm on Highway 258 in 1960. (Courtesy of Mary Alice Johnson Mills.)

with us at the Foxhall farm. She died from throat cancer, and it was a horrible death because at that time there was no radiation treatment for cancer patients. They just kept them as comfortable as possible, with drugs, until they died. The next death to really impact my life was my step-father who died in 1975. He was a father, not just a step-father, to my brother and me. I was devastated. I really loved that old man.

One of my favorite relatives was my Aunt Annie. She has six children and because Mama only had the two of us, I spent a lot of my childhood at her house. She was like a second mother to me. One of her children, Anna Blanche Dew, who is the same age as me, was like a sister to me. When we were very young my grandfather called me Honey and Anna was called Sugar. It was later shortened to Hon and Shug. These nicknames have followed us all through our lives. Before my mother married Walter Dew in 1941, we lived in town with my grandmother on Water Street where the Albemarle is presently located. After the marriage, we moved to the country. At that time and place, there was no electric lights nor indoor plumbing. Later we moved to the Foxhall farm, which was about a mile closer to town, and there we had electricity but no running water. We got water from a well and used an outhouse. I remained there until I was 18 and a high school graduate.

Farm Life

While living on the farm, I went to school and in the afternoons would help out on the farm. During the fall, we would shake peanuts and put them on stacks. Later the thrasher would come to the farm and separate the peanuts from the hay. During the summer, I would chop cotton. When the cotton crop was ready, pickers would come to the farm to harvest it. The pickers would go down the rows with a long sack and pick the cotton from the plants. They were paid by the pound and paid at the end of each week. I learned to weigh the cotton and keep records of how much was picked and by whom. I would put in tobacco, which meant that the men would go through the fields and pull the tobacco leaves off of the stalk, put them into a truck, and bring them to the barn. At the barn,

Tied tobacco was placed in piles to await the sticking up process. (Courtesy of ECML.)

a crew would have what is called a looper and handler. The handlers would hand the looper a few tobacco leafs and the looper would string two or three leafs on a tobacco stick. Then they were put in a tobacco barn and cured. Then it was taken out of the barn and graded. At that time each tobacco leaves was separated into a grade. Each leaf was separated. Then the leaves where tied together. Then the cured tobacco was put on sticks and pressed together. Then they would take the tobacco to market when it opened in the fall. I did this until I got married, graduated from high school, and moved away from the farm.

Living on the farm we had many animals, both for food and as pets. We had mules, hogs, chicken, and dogs. The dogs were used to catch hogs. When the dog would catch the hog, somebody would shoot the hog, cut his throat so that it would bleed out. Then we would put the hog in boiling water and take to hair off. Then we would gut the hog, let it hang somewhere over night. We killed hogs in winter to preserve the meat because we had no refrigeration. The meat was salted and put into the smokehouse to be cured for use during the coming months. The fat was cooked down to make lard for frying and making biscuits. We had eggs and meat from the chickens and milk from the cows. We would let the milk set up over night so the cream would rise to the top. The cream was skimmed off and made into butter.

Married Life

While going to the dances, I met my first husband, Andrew Christenberry. In December 1949, we went to Emporia, Virginia, and got married by a justice of the peace. The reason we did that was because I was under 18 and back then, in North Carolina, an 18-year-old could not get married without parental consent. We told the justice of the peace that I was 21. We got married, came back home, and I went back to school after the Christmas break. We never told anyone about the marriage until I graduated in June of 1950. After graduation my husband and I moved out on the Oak City highway until we got a chance to rent an apartment in town on Granville Street. Later we bought a house on Johnston Street. We were living in this house when our first child, a daughter named Julia Dianne was born. When my husband decided he no longer wanted to work at Long Manufacturing, we sold the house and moved to a farm owned by my step-father. There our second child, a boy named William Earl, was born. After that we had the opportunity to rent a farm from Dr. James G. Raby, which was bigger and there would be more money. When we quit farming, he went to work at a service station in Pinetops. Since Dianne was in school in Tarboro, we lived in Tarboro and he commuted daily to Pinetops. We had C H. Powell build us a house. It was finished in 1962 and we moved in. I have been in this same house every since. My first husband died in 1963.

Later in Life

After high school, I went to work at Runnymede Mills as a folder of socks. When I was pregnant with my first child, Dianne, I quit work and did not work outside the home, except on the farm, until my second child, William, was born. When he was three years old I started work at Security Loan Corporation three days a week. As the company grew I started to work five days each week and stayed there until 1975 when I went to work for Tarboro Redevelopment Commission and became a public housing manager. In June 1977, after raising two children, getting them both through high school and one through college, I married Cecil "Pete" Mills. In 1979 I stopped working due to health problems. In October 1979, my first grandchild, Pamela, was born with severe medical problems. Since I was not working, I was able to stay home and take care of her and her sister, Ashley. I have not worked outside the home since June 1979.

Mary Alice Johnson and Andrew Christenberry were married in December of 1949. (Courtesy of Mary Alice Johnson Mills.)

Dianne Christenberry and William Earl Christenberry are pictured during the summer of 1959 (Courtesy of Mary Alice Johnson Mills.)

Patsy Shelton is shown with her family at Windy Point in 1977. From left to right are (front row) Patsy and Sara; (back row) Ben, Hugh, and David. (Courtesy of Patsy Shelton.)

Sarah Laughlin Shelton ("Patsy"), mother of retired chairman of the Joint Chiefs of Staff Gen. Henry Hugh Shelton, was born March 17, 1917 in Edgecombe County. Her home is about two miles north of Speed, North Carolina, where her husband's family settled and farmed. Interview by Dee Long, May 11, 1999.

Early Memories

I was born on Park Avenue in Tarboro. I was named Sarah Ross for my maternal grandmother. They call me Patsy because I was born on St. Patrick's Day. We lived on St. Patrick's Street, too, at 1107 St. Patrick Street. The house was halfway between Tarboro High School and Bridgers Elementary School. It was a white, wood, bungalow type. We walked to school and went home for lunch. I lived there until I married Hugh Shelton in 1939. My mother lived there until her death in 1988.

During my early years I attended Bridgers Elementary and Tarboro High Schools. My favorite teacher was Miss Clark who taught second grade at Bridgers. She was young, pretty, and sweet.

When I was a child, I played all the time with somebody. Elizabeth Liles lived across the street in Tarboro with her grandmother, Mrs. R.A. Stancil. I remember playing dolls, outside games, and board games.

We did most of our shopping at W.S. Clark's in Tarboro. We bought our groceries from Mr. O.O. Boykin, who delivered. Later, they came from A&P and Pender Grocery. Pender Grocery was where the Marrow-Pitt Record Shop was and now On-the-Square Restaurant is. Cook's Drug Store was on the ground floor of Concord Lodge. It was located catty-cornered from Adler's Department Store. Cook's Drug Store was later Moore's Drug Store. There's a sign that tells about George Washington sleeping there.

Let me tell you about visiting the doctor when I was a child. Whew! Scariest thing! Dr. Will Thigpen delivered me. He was our doctor until 1927. Then we had Dr. Raby. When we were small, he always came to our house when we were sick.

Medicines that I took as a child were aspirin and calomel when they thought I had malaria. I never had malaria! I took Fletcher's Castoria, but not Grove's chill tonic. One time I was sick and became worse. Daddy said, "What you need is a good dose of castor oil." I asked if there was anything you could put in it to make it taste better. He put it in orange juice. I kept it down until I ate candy. All of it came up. I never took castor oil after that.

The way we killed chickens at home was to wring their neck. Wham! . . . just like this.

For breakfast, we had bacon, egg, cereal, toast and milk. Milk was delivered from the Milk Plant in Tarboro every day. Ten quarts were $3.00 a week. A little bottle of milk sold for 5¢. My father would take my brother and me to the Milk Plant. When they started making chocolate milk, that was a real treat.

Sometimes we had tea. Mother was a coffee drinker. We had lots of vegetables and South Carolina cornbread. That's cornbread that's thick, sweet-like cake.

W.S Clarks & Sons was a department store in Tarboro. (Courtesy of ECML.)

Mother's Cornbread:
1 l/2 c. cornmeal
2 Tbs. Sugar
l/3 c. self-rising flour
1/2 tsp. baking powder
l l/2 Tbs. melted shortening
2 eggs
1/4 tsp. salt
Combine all ingredients. Then add enough milk to make a medium batter. Pour into greased pan. Bake in a hot oven.

In the hot summer, we ate sandwiches and what was left over. Every morning, Amos, a black man, came by pulling a cart with homemade rolls for supper. We bought those. Mr. Will Godwin from Mildred came by in his car, which was just filled with fresh vegetables. We bought from him. We had a garden, cow, and chickens. Rhode Island Reds and Leghorns were some of the kinds of chickens.

For lunch, we always had dessert. I always liked "stickies." They were biscuit dough with brown sugar rolled up with butter on them and sliced. We had the biscuit type strawberry shortcake. Mother cooked until I was in high school. Then we always had a cook.

After we did our jobs at home on Saturdays, our group would hike out at 10:00 a.m. Folks don't dare do it now, but we would go through the woods to Lloyd's sandpit behind what is now Martin Middle School. We would take lunch-pickles, Vienna sausage, cookies, and coke or orange crush. Boys and girls went. We had the *best* time.

I got a bicycle when I was 12. We rode to Leggett. There weren't too many cars on the road then. We would get something at Lawrence's Store and ride back to Tarboro.

I had a golden retriever named Taffy. She lived for nine years. My sister had a fox terrier dog, too. My father used the veterinarian services of Dr. O.H. Graham. That's who I used, too. One unusual pet I have is a clock that tweets like a bird, which my sister gave me.

On Sundays we attended Sunday School and regular church services. That afternoon we sat on the porch and talked. Mother frowned on playing cards and going to the movie on Sunday. We played. At 6:00 p.m., we went back to First Baptist Church for BYPU, The Baptist Young People's Union. At Tarboro's First Baptist Church, I was in the first group to be baptized. We let the Chinese girl named Wong be baptized first because she was Chinese. Her daddy ran a laundry in Tarboro. The church building had just been completed. There were chairs in the sanctuary because all the pews were not in yet. My brother, M.L. Jr., was in this group, too.

About 1932 or 1933, I was in the First Baptist Church when Dr. Joseph L. Peacock was pastor. He grew up in Paisley, Scotland, and pastored Thomas Coats Memorial Baptist Church. We went there, too.

I played music in my Tarboro church from ages 12 to 19. I have served as organist at Speed Baptist Church for 60 years, since 1939. I have played since 1936 in all. Mrs. Susie Pender taught me how to play the piano. Then I took at East Carolina from Miss Correll when I was a student there.

One particular Christmas I remember was when we drove to Blacksburg, South Carolina and spent Christmas with my Grandfather Williams. This was about 1929.

Santa Claus brought whatever I wanted—dolls, clothes, watch, bicycle.

For fun, my daddy enjoyed the beach the most. He went with men on fishing trips and came home "tired out." After going to the beach in 1956, he came home on a Friday and died in his sleep on Sunday night of a heart attack. We always went to Kure Beach, Wrightsville Beach, or Nags Head as a family every year until his death.

The Edgecombe County Fair was in what is now Fairview where all the houses are. It was a hot item. Everyone went for the whole day. We got so much money to spend. Our parents took care of the baby and I took care of all the other children. We always bought a basket of apples. I thought it was a funny thing we all *dressed up* for the fair. We did not come home until night, after the fireworks.

My first memory of work was when I was 16, nervous, and enjoyed working at McCrory's Dime Store in Tarboro. This was the first money I made. I made $18.00 weekly in 1932. That was big money. At 17, I worked at Belk's in the summer before going to East Carolina Teachers College.

Siblings

My parents had five children. I am the oldest. Maurice Jr. was born after me. I called Maurice Jr. "Buddy." After three years at N.C. State, he worked for NASA at Langley Field, Virginia, doing testing. Mary Vanice taught private music lessons for piano and organ for 40 years. She was the third child born. Next came Robert Chalmers who graduated from N.C. State as a chemical engineer. He worked for the army at Fort Lee when he got out of service. We called him "Cham." Both he and M.L. Jr. were drafted in the service. Cham attended Wake Forest Southeastern Seminary and became a minister. He had several churches in Virginia. Two jobs got to be too much, so he was only working for the government when he died in 1984. Ethel Mae, the youngest, was an opera singer in New York. She died when her Raleigh home burned in 1995.

My brother was named after my father. Robert Chalmers was named for our grandfathers. Mary

Patsy Shelton sits dressed for a formal occasion with her sisters and mother (Courtesy of Sarah Laughlin Shelton.)

Venice was named for my father's mother, Margaret Vanus Rollins Laughlin. Ethel Mae was named for two of my mother's sisters.

Parents

Daddy was the Edgecombe County Manager. He was the Tax Supervisor and Auditor of Edgecombe County. He borrowed money for the county. The building that is now the Edgecombe County Social Services Building was built during the time he managed Edgecombe County finances.

My family supported the Democratic political party because it was felt that the Democratic Party did more for the people.

My mother was Baptist and my father was Methodist.

My family were very opposed to tobacco and alcohol, even having one beer. They were not opposed to others using them. Daddy chain-smoked, but he quit after his heart attack. He did not want his sons to smoke.

There is never a night my parents found out we were not good. They took no excuse.

For recreation, my mother enjoyed the Edgecombe Garden Club, United Daughters of the Confederacy, looking at antiques, and day shopping trips with friends.

My mother was Mary Irene Williams and grew up in a little town called Blacksburg, South Carolina. By September 1988, she was bed-ridden and needed around-the-clock care so I put her in the Albemarle Health Unit. On October 4, her kidneys failed and she was put in the hospital. She couldn't digest food so a feeding tube was put in her stomach. Dr. Vick called and said she was much worse. When I got there, she had passed away. My mother died the 13th of October, 1988. She enjoyed life and loved her family, friends, and the First Baptist Church.

Teaching and Community Activities

In 1936, I got a two-year certificate from East Carolina Teachers College. I went back to East Carolina University to earn a B.S. degree in primary education. My father paid for two years of the education. The other was paid for by a National Science Foundation Scholarship. I went in summers and on Friday night for the last two years.

From 1936 to 1948, my first teaching job was at Speed School. I took Mary Louise Lawrence's job. She married Joe Edmondson. Since I could teach music, I was hired. I taught first grade and public school music.

The next teaching job was Hobgood Public School, 1952–1955. They did not have a high school. The high school students went to Scotland Neck High School. From 1955 to 1969, I taught at North Edgecombe School. From 1970 to 1981, I taught second, third, and sixth grades at Coker-Wimberly Elementary School. In 1981, I retired.

One community activity that I have participated in is being treasurer of the Edgecombe-Nash Retired School Personnel organization at one time. Also, I have participated in the Edgecombe Garden Club, United Daughters of the Confederacy, and church.

Roles have changed for women. I worked outside the home for 35 years. I still think the husband and father should be in charge. If a woman works outside the home and doesn't neglect her children, it's okay.

Married Life

Meeting my husband wasn't formal. We knew each other as children. My father was Edgecombe County Manager. My husband's father, Mr. Ben Shelton, was chairman of the Board of County Commissioners. When I was about 12, we would come out here. Mother would visit Mrs. Shelton. All the family would come, just to have something to do. All the children played. Later, I was teaching at Speed. He was going to Campbell College. We would date, going to dances and picture shows.

When our son, Hugh, was four years old, my daddy worked at the old courthouse. He drove there

Retired Gen. Hugh Shelton is the former Chairman of the Joint Chiefs of Staff. (Courtesy of the U.S. Government and Edgecombe Community College.)

with Hugh. He was not to get out of that car while his Granddaddy went into the courthouse. Hugh got tired of waiting. He got out of the car and went across the street to George Howard Fountain's office. He said, "I'm looking for my grandaddy." "What's his name?" they asked. "Granddaddy," Hugh replied. "Well, where does he work?" they asked. "At the courthouse," said Hugh. Then they took Hugh to the courthouse where he found Grandaddy. He was the apple of his eye.

When David and Hugh were about two through six, my daddy would read the *New York Times* to them. They thought it was great. They are my two oldest sons.

The most frightened I've been was when it had been snowing and there was one inch of snow on the road. A friend and I were going to Tarboro. David, our four-year-old son, fell out of the car. We were going 50 miles an hour. He made no sound, but the back door made a crackling sound when it opened. It was a Chrysler car and the back doors opened to the front with a handle. I turned around and it looked like he was a mile away, just rolling and rolling. He was bundled up, wearing leather gloves and corduroy pants. The gloves and pants were all torn up. He had brush burns on his arms and legs. I carried him to Dr. Bass every day for treatment. He used penicillin.

There were polio epidemics in the late 1940s. I had three children—Baby Sara, Hugh was eight, and David was six. My sister's little girl got polio and was sent to the Polio Hospital in Greensboro. She stayed until infection time was over. We canceled vacations and stayed as close to home as we could. There was a child on the farm who had polio. It was so prevalent I was frightened to death. My sister's oldest child had therapy and is fine now. My older children took a shot. Ben took the sugar cube. He was born in 1956.

I want my children and grandchildren to get a college education. My parents wanted me to get a college education.

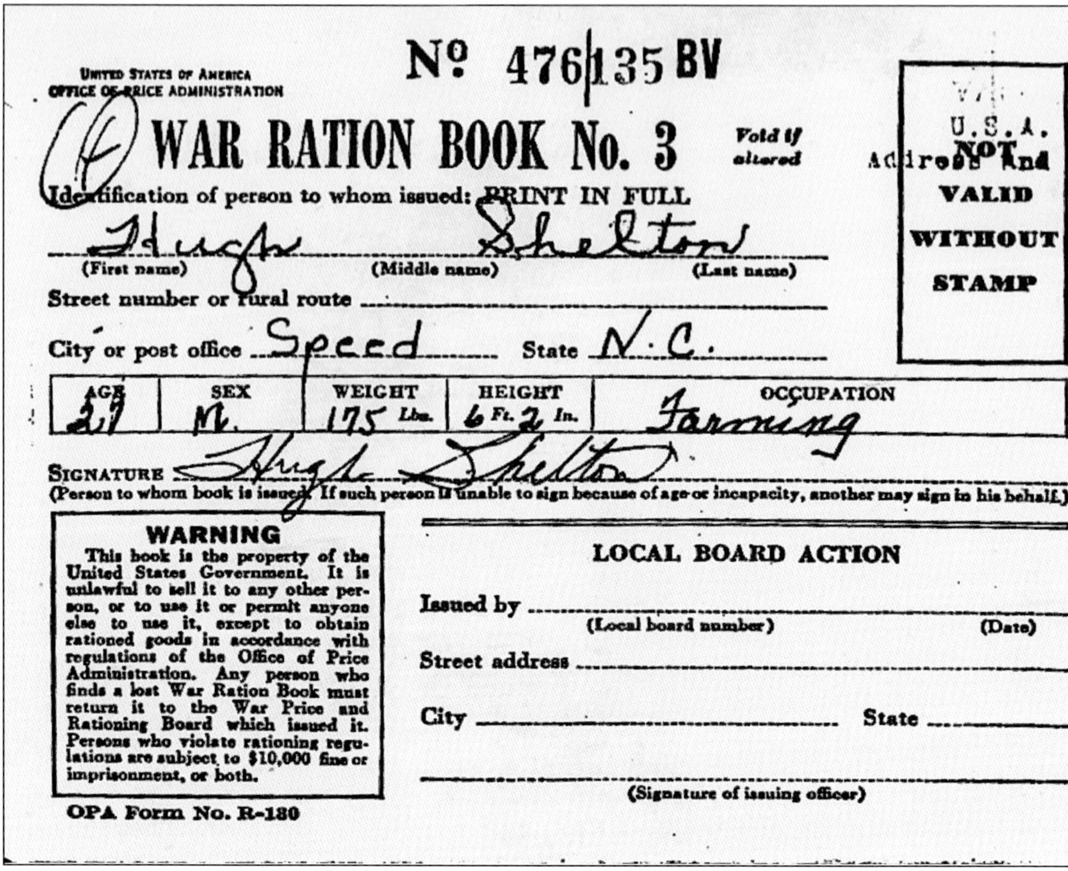

UNITED STATES OF AMERICA
OFFICE OF PRICE ADMINISTRATION

Nº 476135 BV

WAR RATION BOOK No. 3 — Void if altered

NOT VALID WITHOUT STAMP

Identification of person to whom issued: PRINT IN FULL

Hugh Shelton
(First name) (Middle name) (Last name)

Street number or rural route ....

City or post office Speed State N.C.

AGE	SEX	WEIGHT	HEIGHT	OCCUPATION
27	M.	175 Lbs.	6 Ft. 2 In.	Farming

SIGNATURE Hugh Shelton
(Person to whom book is issued. If such person is unable to sign because of age or incapacity, another may sign in his behalf.)

WARNING
This book is the property of the United States Government. It is unlawful to sell it to any other person, or to use it or permit anyone else to use it, except to obtain rationed goods in accordance with regulations of the Office of Price Administration. Any person who finds a lost War Ration Book must return it to the War Price and Rationing Board which issued it. Persons who violate rationing regulations are subject to $10,000 fine or imprisonment, or both.

OPA Form No. R-130

LOCAL BOARD ACTION

Issued by ....
(Local board number) (Date)

Street address ....

City .... State ....

....
(Signature of issuing officer)

War Ration Books were issued during World War II. (Courtesy of Sarah Laughlin Shelton.)

These are the occupations of my children: Hugh is a general in the army and chairman of the Joint Chiefs of Staff. David is a biology teacher at North Duplin High School. Ben is a veterinarian in Williamston. Sara is a third grade teacher at Farmington Woods Elementary School in Cary.

World War II, Hurricane Hazel, Ghosts

I remember the day the Japanese bombed Pearl Harbor just like yesterday. We had gone to church at First Baptist in Tarboro that morning. Afterward, my husband and I went to my parents' home for dinner, and we heard the awesome news on the radio. I remember the day Franklin Roosevelt died, too.

A ration book was issued to a child the day he was born. We had books for sugar, gasoline, and tires. Those who registered 1A were called in the military first. My husband was a farmer and we had two small children, so he was a 1B or 2A, I forgot which. However, I still have his 1941 registration card. I keep everything.

I remember the day World War II ended. We had a radio and I had been outside with Hugh and David. Hugh was playing and I was pushing David in the carriage. The radio was on night and day. When I went inside and heard the news and celebrations going on, it was unbelievable.

The day Hurricane Hazel struck Edgecombe County, the children were at Speed School. I was teaching at Hobgood where I taught for three years. We hadn't heard anything. It was rainy when we went to school that morning. By lunch, a call came from Halifax that we should be on our way to get the children. Those who lived in town went home. We were told to stay in a safe place. I went to Speed and got the children and went back to Hobgood School. My husband stayed home because he was scared of what would happen to things at home. Hugh, my husband, said the screen door blew clear across the yard when he opened it.

No one in the family has ever told me he or she had ever seen a ghost or anything else they couldn't explain. I stopped in my tracks twice when I saw flashes of my father soon after he died and of Hugh, our son, when he was in service in Vietnam. There were no clear features, but it was his shape.

Scottish Ancestors

My ancestors on both sides came over from Scotland. My great grandfather was Doctor Penn Laughlin and fought in the Civil War. Doctor was a name, not his profession. He came from Scotland to western North Carolina. All of my father's people settled east of Asheville, North Carolina around Burke County.

My mother was Mary Williams Laughlin. She descended from the Crawfords. We also visited Crawford, Scotland. James and John Crawford landed in Charleston, South Carolina, where they settled. I am a descendant of James Crawford. My maternal great grandmother, Araminta Crawford, married Weldon Williams and their son, Chalmers, was my grandfather.

Castle Lachlan is six miles south of Strachur in northern Scotland. It is still in my family. MacLachlan Castle was the Scotland spelling. The "Mac" was dropped. In 1800, a new castle was built in site of the ruins of the old castle. The castle and farm went to the oldest son. He lives there now and is head of the clan. I have been there. I have never been so cold. I was shaking even though I was wearing a wool sweater, blazer, and coat with a wool lining. It is on Loch Fyne. My sister, Mary Vanice, and her husband, Jim, and I spent two weeks in 1997 touring England and Scotland.

I'm just happy with no serious illnesses and a healthy family. Late in life I got essential tremors, but I haven't had them long. They just crept up on me. I never long for "the good ol' days." I've had a great life.

Lee R. Hall served as the superintendent of Edgecombe County Schools in 1974. Both Southwest Edgecombe High School and North Edgecombe High School have sport complexes named in his honor. (Courtesy of Lee R. Hall.)

Chapter Three
Professionals

Lee Rawlings Hall was born July 16, 1929, and has had a long career in education, serving at various times in the Pasquotank, Bertie, and Edgecombe County school systems. He is a retired Edgecombe County School Superintendent. On January 24, 2002, Lee was chosen as the Distinguished Citizen of the Year for Edgecombe County by the Tarboro-Edgecombe Chamber of Commerce. Interview by Dee Long, October 31, 2001

My name is Lee Rawlings Hall. I have lived in Tarboro since I came to Edgecombe County and became Edgecombe County School Superintendent.

The Family Home

I was born in a place called Whittey Field. It's a place very similar to where my good friend, Cecil Long, was born in that it was about as far back in the country as you could get. It was up a little lane, a good ways away, about two miles from the Highway 17—a dirt road went up there. I remember that we had a car in Whittey Field, but in the wintertime, the roads were so bad the car couldn't go out. On Saturday mornings, we would hook the mules up to a double-single tree and tie that to the front of the car. Someone would ride or lead the mules, and they would literally drag the car out to the highway. We would tie up the mules out at the highway at a place called Lee's Chapel Methodist Church. It was right on Highway 17. Then we would go to New Bern. When we returned from New Bern, we would hook the mules back up to the front of the car and would literally just drag the car a mile and a half back where we lived, because the roads would get so muddy. There were no motor graders or nobody filling in ruts in those days.

The house we lived in was a moderate farm home at that time. It was totally an A-frame house. There was a back porch with a hand pump. I can remember that some of the prettiest flowers I ever saw grew under that pump. We moved from there when I was about eight years old. My father was disabled during World War I. We moved to Pollocksville because my father was getting more and more disabled. We were able to buy one of the nicest homes in Pollocksville.

Memories of Work

My very first memory of work was when I worked in the garden with my mother. My father could do very little in the way of physical labor which means that by the time I was eight or nine years of age, I was somewhat the "man of the house." By that, I mean if the roof leaked, then it was up to me to crawl up on the roof and fix it because my father could not. If someone brought heater wood in, either my mother or I did it. My mother had four children. She was busy washing, ironing, cooking, and doing things like that. Before she died, my mother made the statement, "Son, I never treated you fairly because I made you the man of the house when you were still a boy." I feel it made life so much better in every kind of way, working and doing everything around the house that had to be done. We always had a cow. From the time I was about eight years old until I went off to college when I was 17, I milked the cow twice a day. "Old Red," great big old Guernsey cow, would fill up a ten-quart water bucket with milk twice a day.

I earned money in a lot of ways from the time I was seven or eight years old. There were some huge blackberry patches behind our house. I would pick blackberries and carry them to a little store that was at the end of our road. I would sell blackberries by the quart for maybe 10 or 15¢. Then my grandfather lived with us. My grandfather had a peg leg. He would make arrangements with people to clear cemetery lots. He would ask me to help him clear them. He would give me a portion of what he was getting paid. My mother would also let me sell some of the leftover milk and cream since I milked the cow everyday, to pick up a little money. I have always been able to make money.

I always loved manual labor. Unfortunately, my hands show it; I never had the hands of a school superintendent.

School Years

I always went to Alex H. White High School in Pollocksville. The school was named after a principal who had served the school very long and honorably. Back in those days, even though it was a grade 1st through 12th school, they were always referred to as a high school. They were union schools, but no one ever referred to them by that name.

I had many favorite teachers. I loved them for different reasons but I had one special teacher. Her name was Julie Whitted. She taught the fifth grade. I always wanted to please Miss Whitted. Incidentally, she lived to be 99 years of age and just died several years ago. I guess my claim to fame from Miss Whitted is that at the top of my report card, she wrote "a splendid student." I still have the report card. That was one of the nicest things that a non-relative had ever said about me.

I went to East Carolina University and graduated with an AB degree in business education. After I returned from the air force, I went back to East Carolina University and got a Master's degree and a principal's certificate. Several years later, I went to the University of North Carolina at Chapel Hill and earned the advanced superintendent's degree.

Going to Town

My family shopped in Pollocksville where we got the staples. The staples consisted of flour. We ground our own cornmeal. We had our own hogs there on the farm. We had our own cow but bought salt and pepper. We had our own lard from killing hogs. We used to buy molasses. You had to carry your own gallon jug down when you bought molasses. At Mr. Armstrong's store, there was a 50-gallon drum of molasses in the back of the store. It was a wood container of molasses up on a little rack. You would turn that little wood spigot, fill up your gallon jug, and take it home. We went to New Bern to buy clothes and other items. Some Saturday afternoons we would get to go to New Bern—"town." That was always a big deal when we got to go to New Bern. Pollocksville was a very small town, a little larger than Leggett perhaps.

Food and Staples

We ate everything. As I think about it now, we always had plenty of good food. My mother would can from the garden every summer. She would can 400 or 500 quarts of different produce from the garden, including blackberries I picked. She would make these great big huge pots of vegetable soup and canned it in half-gallon jars. I remember coming home from school and there was always a "boiled pot" on the stove. It was collards, or beans, or some kind of vegetable in that pot. It usually had some meat from the smokehouse. You would wait until it turned cold weather because you didn't have freezers. Then you would kill the hogs. You would put part of them in salt in a barrel—a layer of salt, layer of meat. Then you would take your hams, shoulders, and sausage, and so forth. You would make up this sage recipe and rub this on your meat, getting in the crevices, too. This prevented insects, worms, and flies from invading your meat. It was a repellent to them. Then you would take it and you would put it up in your smokehouse to dry and to smoke. The recipe was sage, pepper—I don't remember what Mama mixed up. You very slowly would keep just a little heat and a little smoke until this meat was cured. Once it was cured, it would last a year or two. You could leave it in the smokehouse. It would be good all summer long.

We had two ways that we could kill chickens. I was the one who killed the chickens. Sometimes, I would wring their necks. Just grab the neck of the chicken and just "crank." Some other times I would put my hand right over the chicken's head and place it on a chopping block. With an axe in the other hand, I'd chop the head off.

On Saturdays, I usually cut wood when I was growing up. We always had several stoves. Back then, they didn't have power saws or anything like that. We would trade work with my uncle or get someone to help me and we used the crosscut saw. We sawed all the heater wood for cooking. We would go find us some nice pine trees and we would saw these blocks of pine-stove wood. A really good husband at that time kept plenty of good dry stove wood for his wife, thereby showing great honor to her. If he loved his wife enough, he saw that there was some good dry stove wood always

Lee takes a rest from work in 1945. (Courtesy of Lee R. Hall.)

available. When I say stove, I'm talking about the wood cook stove, not the heaters in the house. One of the other things that we always did was find an old tree stump back in the woods. When we were cutting wood, we would cut what was then called lightwood. It was heart pine. It had lots of oil and sap in it. We would cut that and make little lightwood splinters out of it and bring it to the house. When my mother got up in the morning ready to cook breakfast, she would put just a little paper or something to start it and two or three of these lightwood splinters in the stove. Shortly, she had a roaring fire going for breakfast.

Sundays

On Sundays, we always went to church. My parents were Protestant—Baptist. We went to the Pollocksville Baptist Church and attended Sunday school, church, RAs, all of it. Usually you had visitors on Sunday. I can remember some weekends that we would visit my mother's people. We visited them Saturday morning or about lunch after the chores were done. You always spent the night and the children played. The men gathered outdoors or in the packhouses. The women remained in the house or sat on the front porch and talked. Lot of times, they enjoyed quilting bees and other activities. A big breakfast was enjoyed on Sunday morning. We returned home from church to a big dinner. One thing I remember is that usually there were enough beds provided for all adults. No one ever thought about a child sleeping on a bed. You just got on a pallet on the floor. I don't know if that wasn't some of the best fun I ever had—five or six of us in the living room on a pallet.

Family and Friends

My grandmother on my father's side was a Rawlings. My grandmother on my mother's side and my mother were Lees. Hence, Lee Rawlings. I am an ancestor of General Robert E. Lee

My mama was my best friend, but my best non-family friend was Milton Askew who lived a couple doors from me. I always had so many best friends as I was growing up. Milton and I were closer when we were seven, eight and nine years old, but after that, I always had many best friends. My cousins were always my best friends, too. Cousins loved each other so good back then and saw each other all the time.

My family always supported the Democratic Party. I've continued to register as a Democrat, but I don't always vote in the general elections like that. I guess I am more of an Independent right now than any political party. My father would have voted Democratic no matter what.

My family absolutely frowned on using alcohol. I remember that as part of my growing up. Tobacco was handled differently. Smoking was considered acceptable. Many men smoked pipes and chewed tobacco. That was a way of life back then. They didn't know how dangerous it was. I smoked in my earlier years. In my 40s, I put it down and left it.

My father was from Jones County. His name was Gyp Jones Hall. I think that he probably was gassed during World War I, and this is what affected his nerves. He had something like Parkinson's Disease in that he didn't have control of his extreme joints—his hands, fingers, and feet. He could walk, but he staggered. At that time, they simply didn't have all the medical research and other things that would clearly define what caused all of his injuries. He received a pension for injuries received in the war and drew it until the time of his death. This was primarily what supported our family as we were growing up.

For fun, my father loved to go to ball games. He couldn't drive a car, but a relative usually drove for him. On Saturdays and Sundays, many men went to them when I was growing up. There were little church and community leagues. After becoming of age, I drove for him until I entered college. I wasn't at home much after that time.

I sometimes wonder what kind of attitude I would have had toward life if I had spent my life disabled, but I haven't. I spent it as a very healthy, energetic person.

What we call recreation, my mother never knew. My mother never played a game of golf or went on a trip until later in life when my brother, sisters, and I got old enough to take her. Her recreation was through her children, church, and visits with relatives. As it was breaking day, I would see my mother out in the garden working. One of my earliest memories of her is that on Saturday nights until 10 or 11:00, she would be rolling up and ironing starched shirts and dresses. She was getting things ready for her four children to wear to church the next day. I don't guess all women worked as hard as my mother did. Both women and men did hard physical labor at that time—women in the homes and men on the farms.

I have a feeling that a lot of people's lives have greatly improved in the last 60 or 70 years. For women, life is really much better now. My best remembrance of my mother was seeing her constantly at work—seemingly from daylight until dawn. I adopted that from my mother. I'm happiest now when I'm working 40 or 50 hours a week. She taught me a strong sense of responsibility and a strong work ethic.

My mother was from down in lower Pamlico County. Her name was Golda Lee. My mother and I had a very special relationship. I loved my mama so good. When I became financially able in later years, my mother wanted for nothing that money could buy. When my mother died I was off on a camping trip with my wife. I was informed that my mother had had a very serious heart attack. I was

Lee Hall and his mother, Golda, enjoy Christmas day. (Courtesy of Lee R. Hall.)

in the mountains of Virginia. It would take me at least seven hours to get to New Bern.

The doctor told my brother and sisters that our mother was on a ventilator, but she was brain dead and there was nothing they could do for her. About 11:00 that morning, they took mother off the ventilator. My brother and one of my sisters had agreed to take her off the ventilator, but my younger sister, Myrtle, strongly objected to taking our mother off. The other two and the doctor prevailed. Myrtle said, "I tell you one thing. Mama won't die until Lee gets here."

Well, it was 7:30 that night when I got to New Bern. My mother was still alive. Myrtle told me, "I told them mother wasn't going to die until you got here, Lee." They went out of the room. I said to my mother, "Mother, I appreciate you waiting for me. You can go on." I bent over the bed and started rubbing my mother's shoulders. She died within five minutes. I still cannot tell that story without crying right now.

I met my wife when we were both at East Carolina University. They had a student union here. Actually, it was called the "Y Shop." I was in there with a friend one day. She was in there with a friend, too, and we started talking. That's how I met LaVelle.

I have two children who were educated at the following schools: daughter, Katherine—graduate of Yale Law School; son, Leland—graduate of West Point in electrical engineering.

Christmas

I remember lots of Christmases. Christmas was indeed a happy time in our house. One thing that made Christmas so wonderful was there were always special foods around the house. With

Lee Hall and his wife, Lavelle Parker Hall, attend a high school dance. (Courtesy of Lee R. Hall.)

Christmas, I associate tangerines, dried raisins on the vine, nuts, fruits, and candy—homemade sticks of pull candy that we made. I don't know what ingredients mother put in it to "make it pull." It was also the only time I remember we had oranges. There were always English walnuts and Brazil nuts. We didn't have a lot of money, but everybody always got something for Christmas—air rifle one year, bicycle another, some roller skates another, just things that kids got. We didn't get what kids get now, but we got enough. Christmas continues to be a happy time.

Fairs and Carnivals

We had little traveling carnivals that came through. The first thing I remember is a medicine salesmen who would come through, selling some special kind of medicine that could cure anything. They would set up a little tent in town. They went through town playing a little musical instrument, inviting everyone to come for a free concert. You would go down there and they would have singers and dancers. There were minstrel shows. I was very young when this was happening, but I can remember going to them. As I got in high school, I went to New Bern to the carnivals and rode the Ferris wheels and things like that.

Pets and Animals

I worked with the farm animals like "Old Red," the milk cow. I loved to drink milk, still love to drink milk. I always had some pigs and chickens when I was growing up, but they were to slaughter and eat. I love animals, but I never had time for a pet. I was too busy working. I'm sort of like my mother. I didn't have time for nonessentials.

There were usually one or two dogs around the house, but they were never *in* the house. The dogs were under the house, and they ate the scraps that were thrown out that didn't go to the hog pen.

The services of a vet were only for farm animals. The agriculture teacher would come and vaccinate your hogs against cholera. Back in those little communities, he did a lot of the veterinarian work.

World War II, Military, and Piloting

I remember the day the Japanese bombed Pearl Harbor. We didn't hear about it early that morning. Sunday morning wasn't a time we played the radio. When we went to Sunday school, it was being talked about. We came home, and it was all on the radio then.

During World War II, I can remember the main things rationed were gas, oil, sugar, and meat. We had to have ration cards to buy gasoline and many of the staples that we used in the home.

I remember very much the day World War II ended. I remember VE day and VJ day very clearly. There was much celebrating, happiness, and joy each time. We had horrible losses in Japan as we were taking island after island, but then we were able to drop the atomic bomb. The next day Japan surrendered.

I never fought in a war. I have been in service, but we were not in war at the time that I served my time. I got a commission when I graduated from college through the ROTC program and went in the air force. I was given the rank of second lieutenant and required to serve at least two years in the active military. After my two years of the air force, I came back and served in the Army Reserve and National Guard. I was stationed in Lackland Air Force Base in San Antonio, Texas; Kendall Air Force Base in Panama City, Florida; and most of the time, at Moody Air Force Base in Valdosta, Georgia. I retired with the rank of Captain in the Reserve and went into the National Guard for eight years. I stayed in the National Guard until I finally reached the point I needed to get out because my professional responsibilities were too great.

Probably, the most frightened I have ever been is when I was flying an airplane. I was in Atlanta, Georgia, for a meeting there. My wife, Lavelle, and my daughter, Katherine, had flown down there with me. We got ready to come back. We ran into complete solid clouds, "soup" they call it. You could not see anything, any place. To be able to fly in that kind of weather, you needed to be what's called "instrument rated," and I was not. I was "fair weather pilot." In a few minutes, I realized I was disoriented and totally lost. My wife and daughter wanted to know what was going on. In the air force, they have a called sign of "May Day." That channel is monitored by all airports throughout the country. They answered me very quickly. I told them my aircraft number. They started talking, and told me to just look down at my instruments and not to look outside. By that time, perspiration was pouring all over me. The airport took over and brought me back, right over the end of the runway. In that particular instant, I realized how very easy it would have been for me to have lost my life and assisted in the loss of my daughter and wife's lives.

I used to hear my mother tell about the first time she saw an airplane coming up the Neuse River. They didn't know what it was. It was flying through the air. It was absolutely the talk of lower Pamlico County. She said it was just like a miracle.

Sickness and Medicine

During the polio epidemics of the 1940s, I remember we couldn't go swimming or get in large crowds that summer. I had a second cousin, Nina Bell Broughton, who contracted polio, and it left her with a withered leg. She lived her full life with it.

One medicine I used to take was castoria. I used to say if I could control my destiny, I would never take anymore. One very important medicine I took was castor oil. One took castor oil when he had a cold or the flu. I can smell and taste castor oil right now by just saying the name of it. In the spring, families sometimes routinely gave their children what was called black draught. This was supposed to clear and clean you out for the spring to get you ready to go again. Calomel was taken as a purgative; it just really cleaned out your body when you took it. I can remember my mother used to make what was called a mustard plaster. One of her children would have so much congestion in his chest, he could barely breathe. Mother would make this mustard plaster and put it on a cloth. She put it on your chest and tied it on. You would sleep with it all night like that. It seemed most the time when you got up, your chest was better

I can remember we would get typhoid and smallpox shots. When you got your smallpox shot, you got the big sore up on your arm. You would get the typhoid shots, and it would make your arm so sore that you almost couldn't flex a muscle. You got the typhoid shot every three years.

When we would go to New Bern, I would go to the dentist. He would take a pair of dental pliers and pull four or five of my teeth. They were in there just as solid as they had ever been. I can feel him rocking back and forth and pulling one out and grabbing another one, rocking back and forth, and pulling another one out. I had to have all of my baby teeth pulled to make room for my permanent teeth that were coming. I don't know whether it cost a few dollars more or 50¢ more to deaden, but there was never any deadening used. For years, after I grew up, I could sit down in a dentist's chair and the perspiration would start running down my face just when I sat down. Dentists don't hurt you really, but for years, I really had a mental problem about going to the dentist.

Educational Career

When I was going to college, I never thought I would be a teacher. I pictured myself as an upper echelon sales representative. After I graduated from college, I was waiting for the air force to call me to active duty. My wife and I were living in Ahoskie. The Principal of Mars Hill School, Frances Tucker, offered me a teaching job. I said, "Mr. Tucker, I don't know anything about teaching at all. I'm not a teacher." But I agreed to go down there and meet with him. My wife and I needed the money. I agreed to come and take this teacher's position until I got my call. Well, I got there and started teaching these children and absolutely loved it. The air force call came about six weeks before the end of the year. I can remember my father-in-law saying, "Lee, don't you want to finish out the year?"

I said, "Yes sir, but you know, I have my orders and I have to go."

He said, "Somebody in the barber shop was telling me that you might be able to get some new orders cut if you go to Washington to the Pentagon."

"Well, I might be able to do that, Dad, but," I said, "I don't have the money to do it."

He pulled out a $100 bill, the first $100 bill I ever saw in my life. He said, "Why don't you and Lavelle go to Washington and see what you can do. Use this to cover all of your expenses."

Well, a couple days later I went to Washington and got a new set of orders telling me to report the 9th of June to Lackland Air Force Base. We got out of school June 6.

When at the end of the year the principal was passing out awards, right at the end of the ceremony, he said he'd like me to come up." I went up on the stage. He said, "Mr. Hall, I have been in education most of my life and the senior class and I agree that you are the best first year teacher I have ever known in my career." From then on, I was absolutely hooked on education. That's how I came to spend my life in education.

When I became the superintendent, one of the things that surprised me was the fact there was a feeling that country children did not need, and probably shouldn't receive, the same educational opportunities as were provided for city children. This had been brought about, I guess, because many of the towns had chosen to levy additional taxes usually referred to as city school supplements to help support the educational programs in town. What would happen is, families who lived in the country would do one of several things: send their children to one of the school systems in another town; send their children to a preparatory school or a military academy; or send their children to live with a relative in another city. None of these things was unusual for children who were growing up in the Edgecombe County school district and whose parents wanted them to receive the very best possible education. I found this so inequitable I simply could not accept it as the school leader in Edgecombe County.

We did some pretty drastic things to change this. We organized huge meetings in the courthouse in Tarboro in which we had over a thousand people to meet with the Edgecombe County Commissioners, requesting all students in Edgecombe County be equally funded. This was after our board of education had met numerous times with the commissioners and was completely unsuccessful in getting equal funding. After several of these meetings, the commissioners got with our board of education and agreed to fund every student in Edgecombe County equally. This was a *huge* turning point for us in what we were able to provide for our students both in the way of buildings, facilities, books, instructional supplies, and equipment and also special programs such as art, music, and band that we simply had never had in our county schools.

Over a period of years, we saw our schools continue to improve in quality—in course offerings—to the point I was privileged to serve the Edgecombe County Schools as superintendent of an "above par" school system three of the last four years. The state rated schools "below par," "par," and "above par," depending on a complex system of evaluation. Three of the four years we were "above par" and the other year we were "par." No other system that had boundaries touching Edgecombe County achieved that rank. With our achievements at this level, it was a very wonderful and fitting way for me to exit and retire from Edgecombe County Schools.

Another thing that equal funding brought about was a *tremendous* improvement in our school facilities. We didn't have a Maintenance Department when I came here. Our buildings were in very bad condition. I went to the North Edgecombe School right after I became superintendent. The principal of that school was Cecil Long. Cecil said, "Come with me, Mr. Hall; I want to show you something." There were containers of water upstairs in classrooms frozen solid. Students were sitting in these classrooms and taking instruction. The radiators didn't work. The old windows had so many openings around them the wind would blow right in. I can't tell you how deplorable our facilities were. We tore that building down within the first six years I was here as superintendent, and we built a new North Edgecombe School.

The Edgecombe County Board of Education consisted of the following members, from left to right: (front row) Jasper Proctor; Leslie Holley; Zeb Brinson; and William Brake; (back row) E. S. Massey, assistant. superintendent.; C.W. Mayo; Lee R. Hall, superintendent; A. F. Felton; and Kelly Bynum, assistant superintendent. (Courtesy of Lee R. Hall.)

We had every classroom in Edgecombe County air-conditioned at a time when Tarboro City only had about 40% of theirs, maybe Rocky Mount's 40 or 50%. We had carpet on all our classroom floors. We generally were recognized as having the best facilities of any school unit around us any place. Many wonderful people helped me to do this, many wonderful principals and others. I think it is worth noting that Cecil Long was one of the people who helped build these facilities to what they were.

The schools were guarded by community leaders when we first integrated. In so many cases, the feeling was so strong against integration, you had to protect your facilities against certain segments in the community. One example is the Bullock School over in what is referred to as the West Edgecombe area of Edgecombe County. On the Friday night before we were supposed to open school on Monday, the first day of integration, dynamite was carried up on the water tank and a hole was blown in it large enough you could climb right through it. Dynamite also was put on one side of one of the buildings, which blew a big hole there. It blew all the windows out of the building. We worked all Friday night, all day Saturday, Saturday night, Sunday and Sunday night. At 8:30 on Monday morning, we opened school as planned. It was a scary time. This is a strong example of the violent feeling and actions that went with integration.

I have witnessed some cases of abuse and discrimination against people of opposite races—some that embarrassed me, some that made me ashamed, some that I would ask my Lord why it had to be and why they were treated in such a manner.

There were many sit-ins in the schools during integration. It was a very difficult time because students who were entrusted to your care and who were supposed to be taking instructions and guidance from you were just totally defying your leadership. They would feel they had a grievance of some sort and would get together. It started out primarily as black students who were doing this. Black students would gather around in a hallway and refuse to go to class or take any instructions from anyone. Usually, we were able to talk with them and get a group to meet with us individually and to get the others to go back to their classes. These were very tense, difficult times, particularly for the principals who were leading in those schools. There were a tremendous number of very capable principals during this period of time who gave up school administration because nothing in their background had ever taught them how to deal with situations such as this. In some cases, they simply resigned.

The Edgecombe County Schools had many outstanding achievements. We had the number one graduate at the Naval Academy while I was serving as superintendent. Through the board of education's leadership and the great principals and teachers we had in Edgecombe County, we built a school system that was the envy of other systems. I consider that the achievement of my life's work. In the last few years that I worked as school superintendent, we had students who wanted to transfer from Tarboro, Rocky Mount, and other city school systems into our Edgecombe County schools.

I became Edgecombe County School Superintendent on November 1, 1968, and retired June 30, 1993. At the time of my retirement, I had the longest tenure of any school superintendent in the same school unit in North Carolina. I was very fortunate to have the wonderful people with whom I was privileged to serve. Serving as Edgecombe County school superintendent was one of the huge blessings the Lord chose to bestow on me.

I was blessed that I was able to find the right time to retire. They were consolidating the Tarboro City and Edgecombe County schools. They needed a new superintendent of schools. For me, that worked out well. In the last six months of my service, it was a wonderful period in my life because of the devotion my school system showed me.

I don't long for the good ol' days. Almost all the days have been good ol' days for me. I was fortunate enough to have an occupation that I dearly loved. I spent my life in school work and thoroughly enjoyed being in it. I have had lots of God-given blessings all my life.

Cecil Long was the first principal of the new Southwest Edgecombe High School.

Cecil Earl Long is a straightforward man who remains true to his rural roots. He was born February 8, 1930. He is a retired Edgecombe County Principal and Assistant Superintendent. Interview by Dee Long, January 2, 2002.

Home, School, and Family Fun

I was born February 8, 1930, in Martin County on our 55-acre family farm at Route 1, Jamesville, North Carolina. I am the son of Andrew Mayo Long and Mamie Liza Modlin Long. My brothers and sisters are Stella Marie Watson, William Warren Long ["Buddy"], Fannie Gertrude Holliday ["Sissie"], Monnie Ellsworth Long, Andrew Edwin Long, Mamie Clide Fisher, and Maxine Milligan.

A dirt road led to our house from the highway, which was about a mile away. Fortunately, most of the road was a state road and cared for by the state. In bad weather, the road was very muddy. Since the house was not insulated, it was cold. Only the sitting room was heated. Cracks were in the floor. Between the edge of the linoleum and the wall, one could see hogs and chickens under the house. We had an outhouse at the back of the house and a well about 30 feet from the back porch. We carried in all the water we used.

My older sisters and brothers had to walk to Jamesville to go to school. This was about four miles. During my time, we rode the school bus. We walked the long path to the paved road and waited for it. During the cold weather, we went to the neighbor's house near the road. I can remember my hands hurting and turning red when they got very cold. I drove a school bus in high school.

I attended Jamesville School, which had 12 grades. My favorite teacher was Mrs. Opal Brown, my first grade teacher. She would put her arms around me and teach me to read. She died only two years ago. I enjoyed seeing her at the class reunions.

When I was growing up, the family shopped at Sexton Store and Hardison Store in Jamesville for groceries. We went to Gurganus Store in Williamston for clothes like brogan shoes, overalls, coats, underwear, and shirts. All the children saved their money they earned working in tobacco to buy clothes. Money was scarce. With my 5¢ allowance every Saturday, I bought a chocolate-covered popsicle.

When I was a young boy about six years old, I had to wear corduroy knickers. I hated them. I was so happy when I got older and could wear long pants. My mama made shirts and dresses out of feed bags and flour sacks. Some had very pretty designs.

E.D. Rogers and Marvin Perry were my best friends when I was about six years old. Later, it was Perlie Ange, Clarence Ange, and Carol Brown.

On Saturdays, my friends and I rode our bicycles to see western movies at the Colonial Theater in Williamston. It cost 10¢. We had a good time. In the neighborhood, we played baseball and shot basketball goals. We did chores, too.

One job I had was to walk two miles to Padgett's Store everyday and get a nickel's worth of ice. I brought it home in a tow bag and put it in our icebox. When I walked through the woods, I saved a half mile. Even though you could see many poisonous water snakes crawling around near the path, I went barefooted. Later, I had a bicycle and could ride to the store. I felt the bicycle was one of the greatest inventions ever made.

Mama, Papa, and neighbors talked about ghosts all the time. It scared the daylights out of the children. They said they saw deceased kinfolks in the Cedar Branch Baptist Church cemetery. Some were Grandmama, Grandpapa, sisters, brothers, aunts, and uncles who had white sheets on their heads. They said it made them scared. I used to tell Maxine so many ghost stories she was afraid to go in the house alone during the day.

There were several ways Papa had fun. He liked to go fishing in the Roanoke River at Jamesville and Gardner Creek. Our family ate the fish he caught, which were white perch, herring, rock, and catfish. We fried them and made catfish and rock stew. We used to have the neighbors over and make ice cream in the old freezer.

Papa was musical. When he was young, he played with a musical group in the community. He played the guitar and violin. During the week, he played the guitar while Mama, Mamie Clide, and he sang and others listened. He made a banjo out of a cigar box.

The men neighbors would play setback [a card game] at each other's homes while the women talked.

Papa always cut the boys' hair with manual clippers. He would give men neighbors free haircuts. We did not have electricity or a television until I was in the army.

Mama hated alcohol. Papa liked it. Papa did not mind if other people drank either. We raised tobacco and felt good about it. Papa dipped snuff and some of my brothers smoked cigarettes.

There were whites and colored people who made boot-legged whiskey around my home. Mama said those people were "looked down on."

On Sundays, we went to Sunday school and church. Then the children who had already left home would come to visit every Sunday—Marie, Sissie, and Mamie Clide. Andrew would drop by once in awhile. Buddy came regularly until he went in the army.

My family supported the Democratic Party. To our family, Roosevelt was the greatest! He was President during World War II. My family lived through the Depression. Times were very hard, and there was very little money.

Now my mama's life was the church, children, visiting neighbors, raising flowers, and shopping for flower seeds. My mama had me move the same shrubbery until, I know, it was moved all around the house more than once. Wheels should have been put on it.

When my mother died, I recalled how good a mother she had been. I could always talk to Mama. She always wanted her children right around her.

There were quiltings and pea poppings. Peanuts were popped by hand before there were shellers. When one had to shell with their naked hands, their hands would become sore. The sheller was a great invention! Before it, Papa would bend a small piece of oak wood until it had a U shape. The peanut was put down in the U, the legs of the U squeezed, and the peanut shell popped. These peanuts were not just to eat but used as seeds for planting the next crop. Neighbors would go from house to house to help each other. This was a social event, but it was very important. We had an Airedale, a hunting dog named "Big Boy" for a pet. When I was about seven, Papa started giving me the runt pig of the litter every year. I named every one of them "Johnny," even though sometimes she was a female pig. They followed me around all the time, but not anyone else. I held biscuits up high and Johnny jumped up and snatched them out of my hand. Once I gave one runt a whole package of worm medicine. I had decided he might be a runt because he had worms. It was so much worm medicine, the runt's eyes turned green. The pig was a pet until I fattened him up and sold him. Then I would buy a bicycle, baseball glove, baseball, school clothes, or something I wanted. That was *my* money.

When I was growing up, the agriculture teacher acted as the vet. However, because of the Health Department law, every year a vet went around Martin County. He came to a Jamesville store to vaccinate dogs for rabies. They charged a dollar.

I remember the Gypsies traveling through the neighborhood. They would steal everything, especially a pig and chickens. Papa would run them off. They came in wagons they lived in. Some of them worked at the fair.

A 12-year old Cecil plays with "Johnny" the pig. (Courtesy of Dee Long.)

When I was growing up, I went to the Martin County fair. It was a big annual event in the fall. We got $5 for working in tobacco. It was fun and our family went every year. We would shoot the basketball or throw the best baseball to win prizes. We rode the Ferris wheel mostly. We came home with candied apples. When we got older, we went with our girl friends but not with the family.

Teenage Years

When Marvin Perry, Merton Hardison, and I were teenagers, we would bum a ride on the "logging train" (freight train) to Jamesville and back. We knew the arrival and departure times. The train went right by Merton Hardison's home, which was about one and half miles from my home. This train took logs to Jamesville. Then they were put on barges for shipment on the Roanoke River at Jamesville. They went to the Pulp Mill in Plymouth.

Some Saturday nights, E.D. Rogers, Marvin Perry, Merton Hardison, and I would spend the night in the woods. We slept on tow bags and heard many scary sounds. Many snakes were in the woods, and it's a wonder we were not bitten. Each boy brought six boiled eggs, bread, and water. We talked and ate practically all night.

Our family had a 1941 maroon Ford car when I was a teenager. Papa would say, "Go only to Jamesville and back. Don't go anywhere else!" He checked the gas and mileage before I left and when I returned. I had taught myself to disconnect and connect it again. After buying more gas, Marvin Perry and I would not only go to Jamesville, but to Williamston and anywhere else we wanted. Often I had to take Maxine, my younger sister, along when I got the car because Papa would trust me if she was there.

In hot weather, Marvin Perry, E.D. Rogers, Merton Hardison, and I cleared the "water snakes" (water moccasins) out of Jack Hole and went swimming without any clothes. Jack Hole was located about two and half miles from my home. It was in the woods, but we could walk down the railroad tracks from Sexton Road to get to it. Andrew, my older brother, used to go swimming there, too.

Many young people enjoyed swimming holes. (Courtesy of ECML.)

One night Perlie Ange, Clarence Ange, Carol Brown, and I were in Perlie's jeep with Perlie driving. We were coming from Jamesville. Perlie was going at a very fast rate of speed, and it got out of control. The jeep spun around and around in the middle of the road. I was *so* scared. No one said anything, but it finally stopped. Then, we continued quietly on down the road.

My first memory of work that I was paid for was after graduating from Jamesville High School at the Hardison's sawmill located three miles west of Jamesville on Highway 64. The job was keeping the sawdust under the chain as the sawdust was being thrown down. It was hard work.

Health and Medicine

We did not go to the doctor or dentist unless something was real serious, and we had no choice because of the expense. If we had a tooth that needed to be pulled, we tied one end of a string around it and the other end of the string on a door knob. Then we slammed the door. There was no money to go to the dentist and keep the tooth. That was considered "such foolishness." However, I was taken to the doctor when I had appendicitis and broke a collarbone sliding into home plate playing baseball in Plymouth.

For a cold, Mama put castor oil in black coffee for us to drink. It tasted terrible! Turpentine was swallowed in black coffee, too. We took Carter liver pills, but I don't know why; Mama told me to take them.

Papa had a special kind of stone called a "snake stone." He would put it on a snake bite for a week to draw the poison out. The stone stuck right to the skin. Then he soaked the snake bite area in water; the water turned green. Papa owned two of these stones which he kept in a jar. They disappeared, and no one knows where the stones are. There were a lot of poisonous snakes around home including rattlesnakes. Papa got bit by a "popaleaf" [copperhead] and almost died. Mama put the snake stone on the snake bite and he was healed. It saved his life. (Interviewer's note: I asked a chemist friend how this was possible. He said the stones could have been pumice which is of volcanic origin. Editor's note: Some of these stones were obtained from the stomachs of cud-chewing animals, such as deer and cows, and consisted of calcium phosphate. They were often called "mad stones" because they were also used to draw out the poison from the bites of rabid dogs. Source: North Carolina Museum of History.)

Jesse Martin, a neighbor, could talk the fire out of a burn. My sister, Mamie Clide, spilled hot coffee on me. Papa took me to the tobacco barn where Jesse Martin met us and talked the fire out, and, sure enough, the wound healed. Mama and Papa believed in this.

Dr. Smithwick would come for a house call in a horse and buggy. He had his office in his home in Jamesville. I was scared of the doctor. Some of the adults had told us the doctor would get us. Maxine and I played behind the smokehouse when the doctor came to see Mama.

Food on the Farm

We ate things raised on the farm and from hog killing. Country ham was a staple. We ate fatback, backbone, squirrel, deer, and once in a while bear meat, "coon," and turtle. Things grown in the garden were collards, onions, squash, sweet potatoes, Irish potatoes, cabbage, and corn. We took corn to town and had it ground into cornmeal. They kept part of it for the payment. We grew molasses cane and put it up for the winter in lard stands. My family caught 1,000 to 1,500 herrings and salted them down (layer of herring, then a layer of salt, then repeated). They lasted all summer. After we dug the sweet potatoes, they were stored in the heated sweet potato house. Mama brought to a boil briar berries I picked. They were so good eaten with a biscuit.

We used lots of sage in our pork stew. The pork stew has liver, pork meat, and cornmeal dumplings in it. My wife calls it, "Martin County stew." We liked collards with backbone and corn mixed with butter beans (succotash). Mamie Clide would make chocolate fudge and chocolate cake;

Mama would make vanilla cookies. Ambrosia cake is still one of our family favorite recipes. Orange juice was poured over the cake which made it real moist. It had raisins in it, too.

This is the ambrosia cake frosting recipe:

Combine 3 c. sugar, 2 big tbsp.flour, 2 c. coconut milk or water. Bring to a boil and cook about three minutes. Add eight large marshmallows; let them melt. Add coconut from two fresh grated coconuts or two bought packages. Bring to a boil. Let it cool and ice the cake.

Maxine and I ate dozens and dozens of jars of canned peaches during the school year. Being starved when we got home, they sure tasted good. We shared a whole quart at the time. Later, when the grapes were ripe, they took the place of canned peaches. Also, a cold sweet potato and a piece of cold sausage were not too bad either.

During the week, it was my job to split and saw wood. The big, black, iron cook stove in the kitchen was a wood cook stove and the house was heated with wood.

Holiday Celebrations

This is the way we celebrated July the Fourth. Papa dug an oblong-shaped hole 12 inches longer than the pig and deep enough to put in the oak wood used to cook the pig. A piece of fencing wire was put over the hole. The pig was killed the day before. At 5:00 a.m. on July 4th, Papa put the pig on to barbecue it, using a homemade sauce recipe. Mamie Clide and I helped. Some neighbors and cousins from Hopewell, Virginia, came for the 12:00 noon meal. No one brought food; my family prepared it all.

For Easter, Thanksgiving, and Christmas, every family member brought a dish of food. Mama prepared a lot, too. We had a dining room table that would only seat six. The men took turns eating first. After they finished, the children ate. Then the women ate, talked, and washed dishes. There was a lot of good fellowship and it made our family very close. About 50 relatives were in our "not-so-big" house at once. At Easter, some would bring Easter lilies or flowers as gifts. At Christmas, everyone watched Mama and Papa as they opened their Christmas gifts.

World War II

I remember the bombing of Pearl Harbor very well. I was in the seventh grade and we were talking about it at school. I wondered what would happen. Robert Rawls, a big boy in the seventh grade, quit school and joined the navy. He lied about his age.

During World War II, they rationed gas, sugar and meat. Papa would buy a stand of sugar and hide it in the barn. They gave us stamps to buy things rationed. The meat ration did not bother us much because we raised our own meat.

I remember German prisoners came to our farm from a camp located in Williamston near the river. Once I had watched them play soccer at the camp. They came on a truck and would stack peanuts. They were nice looking men and one played the piano.

When World War II ended, it was a happy time because Buddy, my brother, was coming home. All I could think about was Buddy coming home. Several months after the war was over, Buddy came in the middle of the night while everyone was sleeping. Mama, Papa, Mamie Clide, Maxine and I were living at home then. We all got up and sat by the stove and talked.

Military Experience

Clarence Ange and I decided to join the army. The air force said they could not take us until a couple of weeks later, which we felt was too long to wait. We joined the army because they would take us tomorrow. I wanted to join for one year, but Clarence said we should either "get in or get out," so we joined for three years, much to my sorrow. Basic training was rough, but I withstood it. When I was in boot camp in Fort Jackson, South Carolina in 1948, I lost some of my hearing, especially in the left ear, on the rifle range. I did not realize this then.

Cecil Long served as a military policeman in Alaska (Courtesy of Dee Long.)

I was sent to Adak, Alaska, for four months. There was not a tree or woman on that Aleutian island. It was *very* cold. Then I was sent to Whittier, Alaska, for eight months. I started unloading ships, and they asked for volunteers for military police. I raised my hand, because that was inside and I could keep warm. When we went to the mess hall to eat, we held each other's hands so none of us would get lost while it was snowing. When it was snowing, the wind would blow the snow like it was a blizzard. It was usually about 16 feet deep, but paths were cleared for us to walk places. The snow removers ran 24 hours a day. The only thing we had for entertainment in Alaska were movies, snow, and ice. I was in Alaska in 1949.

They offered me a furlough for one month. While I was home, I got a telegraph wire stating the Korean War had broken out and to report to Fort Bragg to be sent to Korea. I had been told that if you went overseas for a tour, they could not send you overseas again. I told the Captain this. He said, "Soldier, in the time of war, everybody goes." Now I was on the troop ship again. In South Korea, I could hear the artillery fire. I was in Korea in 1950 through 1952.

The NCO Club had entertainment. Bob Hope came over and entertained the troops. Also, we had dances with Korean girls. I had no complaint about army food in Korea.. However, I did not like Korean food because there was too much garlic in it. Another reason I would not eat it is because if Koreans ran over a dog, they would clean the dog and eat him. I wanted a steak and glass of milk, but Korea did not have any restaurants.

My long-time army buddies in Korea were John Willoughby from Newport News, Virginia, and Robert Reynolds from Moultrie, Georgia. When we felt down, we had a contest to see who could stay happy the longest. John Willoughby would always win.

This was a very backward, poor, and dirty country. It smelled badly because of the human manure put on the rice patties. Women carried bundles on their heads and men carried them on their backs.

I was in the combat engineers and worked as a parts clerk who looked at all parts and their names. They repaired generators, bulldozers, and heavy equipment. I thought I was having fun until the third morning. I woke up and saw a truckload of bodies coming from the front that was headed for the cemetery. I served three years and then got a "Truman year" (editor's note: an extended year). It was time for us to come home. When they asked for volunteers from the company to stay six more months, I volunteered because they promised us sergeant stripes. Then I came home as a sergeant.

Work and Higher Education

After coming home, I worked at Belk-Tyler's Department Store in Williamston for six months. Then I farmed the family farm for one year. I was living at home when Hurricane Hazel struck. Tobacco and corn blew down. The tobacco drowned. It was a bad situation. I made very little money on farming that year.

I didn't like either job, so entered East Carolina University where I majored in business administration and minored in social studies. After graduating with a B.S. degree, I measured land with the North Carolina Department of Agriculture in Pitt County until I was hired as a State Probation officer. Next, I was a guidance counselor at Rocky Mount High School.

Married Life

My wife, Josephine Ardelia Harper Long ["Dee"), was born June 18, 1936 in Edgecombe County on her family farm at Whitakers, North Carolina. I introduced myself to her in the East Carolina Library when she was studying. I liked her looks. I had seen her once before downtown on the

Cecil and Dee Long were married on October 28, 1956; this is their wedding portrait. (Courtesy of Dee Long.)

street in Greenville walking toward the college. Dee and I married October 28, 1956, while we both were students.

We moved to New Bern where all our children were born. Later, I was transferred to Greenville and Dunn. Since Dee's father was not in good health and needed help, we began to make plans to build a house on the Harper family farm, which we owned. In the meantime, her father died, so we moved into the two-story house already on the farm and where her parents had lived. We have three children: Rita Ann Baker, and the twins, Steven Brent Long and Stuart Bryan Long.

Educational Career and Integration

I was principal at North Edgecombe School, West Edgecombe School and Southwest Edgecombe High School. Before I retired, I became an Edgecombe County Schools Assistant Superintendent. It was after teaching at North Edgecombe High School that I became the principal. We moved to the "principal's house" located on the school grounds. Then we moved to our much-loved, beautiful new brick home in Tarboro, North Carolina and have stayed there since then.

It was very rough during integration. After the schools integrated, I witnessed a Klu Klux Klan meeting. They were burning a very tall cross in the front yard where the Lewis and Eason families used to live near our farm on the Leggett-Whitakers highway. This was about three miles from Leggett. You could see the light it produced from way down the road. We rode by and saw a small group standing around wearing white, triangular-shaped, hooded hats and loose-fitting outfits. We did not stop.

Ten members of the Klu Klux Klan visited at the very first North Edgecombe High School PTA meeting. Their leader was a local businessman. After the meeting started, they walked down the auditorium aisle, and the leader said, "Do you want us to show you how to get the n——— out of the school?" Most of the students in this school were black and there were many blacks in the audience. I told the people the meeting was adjourned, and they were excused. The sheriff, whom I had asked to come, was there.

When I was principal at West Edgecombe School, there was a sit-in of about 425 blacks including the black cheerleaders. After I had Nellie Hunter, a respected black teacher, talk with them to find out if their grievances were legitimate, the students went to class. The white coaches were letting white cheerleaders in their offices, but not the black cheerleaders. I resolved the problem. When the coaches were asked how it should be handled, they said, "Call the sheriff." To that, I replied, "There are only about 8 deputies and 425 students." I told the coaches, "The next damn time we have a sit-in for this reason, you will solve the problem yourselves."

The black and white students sometimes fought, but all and all, we got by as well as anybody.

Then I became the first principal of Southwest Edgecombe High School where I retired and became an Edgecombe County Assistant Superintendent.

Retirement Days

If you ask me if I miss the good old days, I'd say, "No! These are the good old days."

I was active in the William and Mary Hart Presbyterian Church of Leggett serving as a deacon and superintendent of Sunday school. I was president of the Leggett Ruritan Club. Now I attend the St. James Methodist United Church in Tarboro where I have served as superintendent of Sunday school and usher.

I want for our children and grandchildren to get a good education, be healthy, have stable homes and a Christian upbringing.

One thing I enjoy is listening to gospel and country music. I never sing. In the car, I listen to the many tapes we play. The radio station is usually tuned to a country music one. I'd rather go to a country music show than to hear the North Carolina symphony play. My wife says when I die, I will go to Nashville, Tennessee, and she will go to heaven because she keeps the religious station on her radio.

Joe W. Dickens Jr., a funeral director, was born September 14, 1953. (Courtesy of Joe Dickens.)

Joe is one of 11 children and the son of Joe W. Dickens, Sr. and Isabelle Knight Dickens. Joe is considered to be outgoing and pleasant and he is popular in our community. Interview by Dee Long, January 1, 2002.

Both my parents and I were born in the Speed area. We lived on Highway 122 between Speed and Tarboro. I married Olga Thornton, and we have two children named Joe W. Dickens III and Jacqueline Marie.

I have served on the Edgecombe County Board of Education. Now I'm on the Board of Directors for Heritage Bank, Council of Aging, and the Tarboro-Princeville Community Development Corporation. I am an Edgecombe County Agricultural Agent but own and manage Dickens Funeral Home, which I started. It is in Tarboro, North Carolina, and is on the Oak City highway. For the last year or so, I have been working with the Princeville Preservation Cemetery folks to try to redo the cemetery there in Princeville.

Getting Started in the Funeral Business

Getting involved in the funeral business was not an easy decision for me to make, especially in the Afro-American funeral business. One either gets in because he was born into it or married into it. I did not do either. I was in the ninth grade when I decided to become a funeral director. I went to several funeral homes trying to get an apprenticeship. During my junior year, I had the opportunity to work with a firm in Greenville. I thought that I was going to get to do my apprenticeship there, but two weeks before graduation, the man told me I couldn't. I offered to work without any compensation. He said that he couldn't do it. My world was crushed.

My guidance counselor got me into A&T, but I never gave up the dream of being a funeral director. I finished my ag. degree at A&T. Later, I completed the program at Gupton-Jones College of Mortuary Science in Atlanta, Georgia. I came back and taught school and did what they call trade-embalming work—embalming the individual in preparation for casket. After ten years of doing that, I decided I was going to start my own business. That's how I got here and have been here now for 15 years.

This building was a country store. My daddy-in-law was a building contractor in Enfield. He redesigned it and made it into a funeral home. It worked out well because it was far enough from town that it was not high-priced commercial property so I could afford it. Everybody said to me that I was crazy trying to start a funeral home and not being in town. I said to them, "I always heard if one could build a mouse trap just a little bit better than anybody else, that the world will make a path to his door." That's been my philosophy. I knew I would have to do some things that other funeral directors didn't do, but it has paid off. People have been very receptive.

Basically, the schooling required to be a funeral director are the science courses—anatomy, pathology. They also want one to know how a business operates and functions. They have embalming courses, funeral directing, and one learns the customs of different people. For example, now that we are having a large Hispanic population, it's important that the local funeral home understand what rituals are used for their funeral services.

Funeral Rituals

There is not a great deal of difference in rituals of the Hispanics and whites. That is not true with blacks and whites. The black service is a celebration. It's usually upbeat music. The eulogy is telling of the good things of the person. It's a service of going home celebration; now you have gone to heaven. It's a little bit more upbeat. You have a little more organizational detail. For example, black families are going to have printed obituaries which are a history of that person. They keep records. It's interesting to see some of the old funeral bills and see the difference in the way funeral bills were written, say pre-1970. Normally, services were a small fee. That is not the case today, because the Federal Trade Commission requires funeral directors to itemize the service charges.

Blacks "funeralize." Whites "have a funeral." There are some differences during the services. Blacks read telegrams. As an Afro-American, if my first cousin died in California, I feel obligated to go to the funeral even if I have to borrow the money. My secretary who is white says, "The person died today. We are having her visitation tomorrow night. We have the funeral Friday afternoon. We'll be free for the weekend." If a black person died on Wednesday, they would not even think about having the funeral until Saturday or Sunday. The big day now is Saturday. The reason is many industries and companies do not allow people to get off for funerals. Therefore, we move them to weekends so all the cousins can come. It's almost a small family reunion.

It is very seldom we have a family who requests gloves as in past years. With black families, you are going to dress and wear your very best. Most times the service will be held in the church. I get more requests now for chapel services than I used to. Regardless of whether the person went to church or not, unless that person left some real strong feelings that he not be taken to a church, he's going to be taken to a church. There will be flower girls and pall-bearers for the funeral. A lot of children are flower girls. It's an Afro-American custom. The visitation the night before is big with Afro-Americans. Basically, that's where everybody goes to socialize and sort of keep everybody happy. If you are the family, you stay up until the wee hours of the morning because somebody is in and out of the house most of the time. They like to bring a lot of food. It's not how much you bring, just the mere fact you brought some.

Then there are different religious customs that we have to be aware of. For example, the Episcopal church uses a pall to cover the casket. This signifies that everybody is equal in the eyes of the church. They do not use flowers on the casket. You will not know whether it's a $5,000 or $300 casket under that pall. In most churches, the remains are placed across the front of the church. One of the reasons it's done is so during the public viewing in that part of the service, they can have the opportunity to look at the person for the last time. In the Episcopal Church, the casket is left perpendicular, straight in the aisle with the head toward the cross so that you don't have to turn the casket. They have Holy Communion, but you don't see that often. Modern-day Episcopalians don't do this. The Episcopalians use the sand to do the committal with. For a lot of other denominations, the funeral director uses live flowers or nothing at all. Episcopal and Catholic churches have a certain burial ritual, so whether you are a United States President or a janitor, you get the same service.

In southern areas, the public still pull their cars to the side of the road and show respect; large cities do not do this.

Funeral Procedures

Information recorded on the deceased's biographical card include birthdays, parent's names, sisters and the brothers, type of work they did, social security numbers, addresses, and the number of grandchildren

You can bury a casket. Vaults have never been required. The reason they sell them is for some form of protection. You don't want to buy a nice casket and then put it directly in the ground. Years ago, all the graves were dug by hand. Today all these graves are dug with some form of backhoe. That equipment plus monument company trucks going across the gravesites and putting down monuments necessitates this extra protection.

For cremation, I would suggest having a viewing with the person first. Cremation is done because it is cheaper for one thing, or the fear of being put into the ground or taking up a space for eternity. A funeral service brings closure. During the last week, one is at his worst. At a funeral service viewing, you see the deceased looking better. Eventually, cremation is going to be more popular, but I suggest cremation be done after the service.

One must be embalmed if there will be a public viewing or no burial in 24 hours or the person dies of a contagious disease. The embalming process is so beneficial. Embalming is done by injection using the artery and veins, the circulatory system.

Normally firms keep hearses for a long period of time. They stay so long at the firm that they become part of the family. They don't want to part with them.

Changing Procedures

Pre-need is one of the biggies now. One mother made pre-need plans for her and her husband. The mother died first. The family had a disagreement over the color pink which one said was her mother's favorite color. The mother had said she wanted a white casket with a light blue interior. The mother had signed a paper saying this. This made an impossible situation possible.

Some elderly people come in to make pre-needs. However, most of our clientele are our age group making the call for a family member. Funeral business is very traditional. If you bury grandmama or grandpa, you bury mama, daddy, sisters, and brothers. Unless somebody gets mad, you don't change a whole lot. We have been able to offer a little better service and, because of our age, attract the calls from younger folks.

At one young person's funeral service, his brother played the saxophone for 15 minutes at the cemetery, just like at a night club in a big city. It was a big tribute. The old ones asked why he had to do all that. Some bring their own music—not that they don't like our music.

Funeral directors where gangs are let the gangs do the final dressing of their members.

You can't get logged into tradition; you must be versatile. Many come in with different ideas about how they want things conducted. You must be willing to do what they want or lose business.

Children at Funerals

Most children are fascinated about the hearse. It's not something they see everyday. When I first started in funeral service, little kids were afraid of the hearse. They didn't want to come near it because they saw it as a death vehicle. Now kids want to know can they ride, can they get inside, can they see inside. There is no fear for the hearse anymore. It's just another pretty, large, shiny vehicle.

Dickens Funeral Home is located near Tarboro. (Courtesy of Dee Long.)

I would say a child should be able to attend a funeral at any age and should not fear it. A child should understand as early as possible that a funeral is a way of life, part of the cycle. Funeral homes now are doing more to help kids understand death. We want kids to view the remains so they can have a better memory picture. A child may go to the nursing home or hospital and see grandmama with tubes in her nose and equipment on her. When the child attends grandmama's funeral and sees her peaceful, smiling, and looking like grandmother, the memory is better.

Funny Stories

A funny thing happened at one service we had. We got to the church that day. All the way in, the daughter of the deceased woman said, "Mama, I'm going all the way. I'm going all the way, Mama. Mama, I'm here. I'm going all the way with you." We came out of the church and she kept repeating it. It was a real cold day. We got to the cemetery and did the committal. She said, "Mama, it's cold out here. I've done gone as far as I can go." The fellows thought that it was mighty amazing that from the house to the cemetery she was going all the way, but that cold weather got her at the cemetery. That was as far as she could go. "I've got to go!"

One woman died at home and the county coroner came and pronounced her dead. He was not professionally trained. A funeral director gave the woman the mirror test. If her breathing fogs the mirror three times, the person is alive. This woman passed the test and was put back on a stretcher and taken to the hospital. She was in a deep coma and lived 10 more years. She always wanted to be taken to him when she really died.

Local Burials and Future Plans

We bury somewhere around 30 or 35 in a year. We are a small firm. We have buried some interesting and well-known people in the community. I buried a fellow whose son put a small bottle of bootleg whiskey in his pocket right before the casket was closed. He said his daddy loved bootleg whiskey. We handled the funeral service for Ada P. Williams, a retired Edgecombe County teacher and principal; Annie Johnson, a retired principal; Karo Bulluck, a building contractor whose wife was a teacher; and Carolyn Powell, a former mayor of Princeville.

I go to the funeral home every evening. I try to spend at least two hours or so there, but if something is going on, or if there is a service, I might be there until midnight. It is just growing at the right pace that probably at retirement, the business will boom, hopefully, and our son or daughter could take over.

Melton M. Caison ("Mel"), a funeral director, was born October 5, 1937. His children are Mel Jr. and Wendy. Interview by Dee Long, January 1, 2002.

I was born in Sampson County and grew up in Roseborough, North Carolina. I started in the funeral business in 1960. I worked as an apprentice with Jernigan-Warren in Fayetteville. I came to Tarboro in 1963 and started working June 1, 1963 at Carlisle Funeral Home. There are three black funeral homes and one white in Tarboro.

I am a member of the Edgecombe County Hospice Board and on the Board of Directors at Heritage Bank.

Getting Started in the Funeral Business

A friend of mine owned a funeral home in Fayetteville. He talked me into going to work with him for awhile. I decided to go to embalming college. I went to Cincinnati College of Mortuary Science in Cincinnati, Ohio, which is a department or division of the University of Cincinnati. They give a funeral service degree. We have to have hours of continuing education every year to renew our license.

You take a national board to be licensed and a North Carolina Funeral Director exam. It used to have two licenses, one for embalming and one for a funeral director. If you are licensed in both of them, you get a funeral service license, which Tommy Dew and I have.

I feel a career in the funeral service is very rewarding, when he feels like he has helped a family and they are pleased. There is no such thing as Saturdays and Sundays off. One has to work just like it's any other day. Holidays are the same way. People don't make appointments to die, but die anytime. One has to be there for that family when something happens. If one can't be there when they need you, they certainly don't want you around later.

The old Carlisle Funeral Home was located on Pitt Street (Courtesy of Mel Caison and Carlisle Funeral Home.)

The new Carlisle Funeral Home is pictured as it appears in 2002. (Courtesy of Dee Long.)

Funeral Rituals and Practices

A wake and visitation is the same thing. In years past, lots of times the funeral home wasn't anything but a storefront. Many times, the funeral home was in a furniture store. You would put the body in the casket and carry it to the home. They didn't have any facilities there for any visitation or service. They would carry it back to the home for the wake that night. It got where they would have the service at the funeral home or church. Then the family would just be at the home the night before. Now the visitations are larger than the funerals because people working can't get off like they used to. That gives them an opportunity to spend some time with the family. They are also beginning to have some night funerals. The family has a visitation from seven until eight. At eight o'clock, they have the service. The next morning just the family and the minister go to the cemetery for the burial. I like to see that rather than graveside funerals. I'm not knocking them, but if the weather is bad—cold or rainy—it's not a very pleasant time. You take elderly people—one must stand for a long time, but you can't provide chairs for everyone. Then the service lasts 15 or 20 minutes. It's hard for some of these older people to stay that long. I have done some funerals in the chapel and no one went to the cemetery. Then the weather is not a concern. The people don't have to stand around so long. In the hot summer time, we have had some people to get too hot at cemeteries. We helped them get back to the car to sit down.

Thirty years ago, no one wanted to talk about making prearrangements for his/her funeral service. Now they prearrange, and pay for it, which is good. Those left behind know what that person's wishes are. Our society has changed. More people want their wishes carried out.

There is more cremation than there used to be. Cremation costs much less. You do not have to purchase a vault, casket, or cemetery plot. There are different forms of cremation. You can have 1. a visitation and a viewing, then a service with the body present, then have the cremation or 2. direct cremation or basic cremation, which is done when the person dies and that's it. We have done several of the number 1 type.

Six or seven years ago in Raleigh several bodies were found in a van that were supposed to have been cremated. After that, some laws passed. The state law is you have to hold a person out for 48 hours before you cremate, to make sure there are no objections or foul play.

There are not that many manufactures of hearses. I would say less than seven. I waited until the end of 1997 to buy and got a bigger discount, but it still was new. I paid about $65,000. The retail price was like $73,000 or $74,000. You can get any color you want. We always use dark blue. Black was used for a long time, but a lot of funeral homes got away from black. A lot of blacks have white hearses. Martha Baker has black; Hemby-Willoughby has white.

There is a law that has just been passed in the last four years that burial has to be 18 inches underground. Before then, there was no law governing this. When all the floods came, vaults and caskets were pushed up. The reason is a lot of the black cemeteries buy vaults instead of buying a marker. They buried the vault cover top right level with the top of the ground so you could see it. Of course, there was nothing to hold it down. Whenever water came in, it would just push that thing right back up out of the ground.

Some cemeteries charge more for digging a grave on weekends, but we do not. We charge $300. We dig graves in Greenwood and all out in the county except at the town of Macclesfield who digs theirs for $400 any day. Edgecombe Memorial Park charges $500, and more on holidays and weekends.

Funny Stories

This was something funny that happened at one funeral service. When I was serving my apprenticeship in Fayetteville, there was a real large lady who was a minister. Her husband was real small. She was almost twice the size he was in height and weight, too. The two used to sing together in funeral services. She played the accordion. They had a service where her husband was a pallbearer. They were down in the part of Cumberland County where it was a real sandy area. In sandy land, they have a lot of problems with graves caving in. What they would do was put boards up around the grave so nobody could fall in the grave and it would be safe. At the cemetery, they told the pallbearers to look and be sure you step on those boards because it's sandy land and it'll cave in. Well, her husband wasn't paying attention and he stepped on the sand. His foot sort of went into the grave. He didn't go in the grave, but his leg did. "Ohhh!" his wife started hollering and called his name. "Ohhh, Heath!" The accordion was loosely hooked and every time she moved, it made a walking sound. The family of the deceased got tickled at her and had to go behind some bushes, but we finally got it straightened up.

Changing Customs

You used to have a lot of services in the homes. They would stay there the night before the funeral. They also have families who set up with the bodies at night. Then you had the service in the home the next day. You buried them in the cemetery right there around the home on the farm.

You don't have many burials in family cemeteries anymore, and you don't have many families now starting family cemeteries. We do have a problem in Edgecombe County. I've talked to the county commissioners about it.

We had a burial on the other side of Speed going toward Hobgood. We had to go in and cut down trees to get the hearse in.

We had several in the last five years that want to start a cemetery on their land. We have had one where the man died and his wife wanted to bury him right back of the house. She had just about a two-acre lot. The county let her do it. She sold the house and moved away.

Farmers start cultivating; they get close to a cemetery. I know in one case, the farmer threw the stones in the woods and just cultivated the whole cemetery. Many family members tracing family history call us to ask where they are buried.

The funeral of Christine Lyde Smith Harper was conducted by Carlisle Funeral Home. (Courtesy of Dee Long.)

Cemeteries can really hinder development. There is a cemetery in the Plaza Shopping Center parking lot in Greenville, and in Wilson in the back of Parkwood Mall. They could never get permission to move them.

Employees and Clientele

We do about 150 funerals a year. I think we operate our business with the least of any funeral home our size. The reason is I'm able to take advantage of a lot of part-time help. Three full-time workers include two licensed, Tommy Dew and me. Charles Fussell is a nonlicensor. The gravedigger is full time.

The most famous burial was when I was in college in Cincinnati, where I worked for a funeral home part-time. We buried the original Superman who had committed suicide in California but was from Cincinnati. His mother didn't think he had committed suicide. She had him disinterred in California. Then she had him transported to Cincinnati. They performed an autopsy, and then had another funeral service which was probably 10 years after he had originally died. His mother thought he had been murdered.

I feel like everybody we bury is famous. We have buried some very prominent people in Edgecombe County and in Fayetteville when I was there.

Carrie Dickens Stanley is a very active senior citizen. (Photo by Minniejo Gay.)

Carrie Dickens Stanley was born in 1933 in Edgecombe County, five miles from Tarboro on Highway 258. Her home was flooded due to Hurricane Floyd in 1999. Her story was recorded at her temporary home in Rocky Mount, N.C. She returned to her new home in Princeville in December, 2001. Interview by Minniejo Gay, ECGS Oral History Chairman, November 29, 2001.

Family and Farm Life

I was born Carrie Dickens in 1933 in Edgecombe County about five miles from Tarboro in the rural area on Highway 258. My father, Joseph Dickens, worked as a laborer with the Atlantic Coast Line Railroad and my mother, Emma Lee Dickens, worked as domestic help on the John Bridgers farm on Highway 258. She worked for the overseer, Mr. Frank Edmondson, who lived in what we called the "yard house." We lived there up until I was about twelve years old. My daddy, Joseph Dickens, bought a house in Princeville and my grandmother, Charity Purvis Dickens, stayed with us. It was like she was the boss of the house even though I had a mother and father. She would do most of the cooking and take care of the children. She did midwifing for her daughters and daughters-in-law. She died about 1947–48 with a stroke and she was diabetic. She had 3 boys and 6 girls and they were all diabetic except my mother who died at 52 with kidney failure.

I had a sister, Mamie Dickens and a brother, Joe Willie Dickens. My sister Mamie was a deaf-mute. When she was about twelve years old she attended the school for the blind and deaf in Raleigh, North Carolina. Mamie stayed at the state school for the deaf until she was about 15 and since she started so late, they said she would have to come out. They had so many small children to come in and did not have room. They said the smaller children could pick up so much faster than she did. She did not go to the school until she was twelve years old, which gave her a disadvantage. Because of having to leave the school she became very nervous, she was paranoid, could not talk or hear and when she would see people talking. She thought they were talking about her and she would fight them. My mother had to stop work so she could be at home with my sister who ended up having a nervous breakdown. She went to bed one day and just would not get up. She stayed in the bed for a year not getting up for anything. My mother had to take her food and everything. Mamie died in 1997 from a stroke while she was in a nursing home.

We worked on the farm. We picked cotton, shook peanuts, and whatever else needed to be done. My brother was sort of a yard boy and worked around the farm house collecting eggs and doing anything that needed to be done. My mother stopped working for Mr. Frank Edmondson and started working for Mr. Albert Battle. She was at the big house and I worked at the log house. That is out near McNair Road and she worked there until she retired.

While we were living in the country, we seldom ever came to town except on Saturday to buy groceries. Someone would hitch up the mules and wagon and pick up everybody that was going to town. They would stay until just before sundown and you would see them coming back from town. Of course, we raised our vegetables and had hogs and chickens, cows, and there was a man that would come on that farm and kill cows about twice a year. The only things we bought were corn meal, sugar, flour, coffee, salt, and stuff like that.

I remember going to town when I was about five or six and that was really something, going to town. We never saw people so dressed up. We would start at the feet looking and go up to the head

The Albert Battle home stands on McNair Road in Tarboro. (Photo by Minniejo Gay.)

The Mose School still stands on State Road 122.. (Photo by Minniejo Gay.)

and back down again. Miss Molly, the boss lady, said she saw Peggy, that was me, down town and she was looking from head to feet, we just didn't dress up that much.

I do not remember going to the doctor but once and that was for a sore throat. The public health nurse gave us our vaccinations.

SCHOOL

I went to school at Mose School, mostly in the spring and winter, because in the fall we had to pick cotton, shake peanuts, and help harvest the crops. We walked about two miles to school by taking a shortcut through the pasture where the cows and pigs were. There were strands of barb wire around the area, and where we climbed through, it was bent down. In the winter, when we got to school, there was no fire. It was a three-room building still standing now on Highway 122, and there was no fire so the larger boys of the class would cut wood and make the fire. We would be crying because our hands and feet would be frozen from walking to school . In the middle room there was a pot-bellied stove and the larger girls would cook on this stove. We would have beans and fried meat. They could not cook biscuits on the pot-bellied stove so they made flour-bread in a pan on top of the stove. We had milk and fruit and we would eat lunch at school. There were five or six classes and we were all in one room. The teacher separated us so that the first class was in the first row, the second in the second row and so on up until we reached the sixth or seventh grade. Of course, we

This section house was home to the railroad overseer at McNair Crossing. (Photo by Minniejo Gay.)

had outdoor toilets at school back then.

I was in about the sixth grade when we moved to McNair Railroad Crossing. It is now McNair Road. My daddy and the people that worked for the railroad had houses there called section houses. We lived there in one of those houses right on the railroad. (Interviewer's note: a section house was preassembled in sections. We call them manufactured homes now. Back then you could order them from Sears Roebuck and Company.)

We went to McNair School. I only had to walk right down the railroad to the school where I went until I was in the seventh grade and then attended Carver School in Pinetops and then we had to walk a mile to catch the bus. I stayed in Carver School until I was twelve and we moved to Princeville.

I attended Conetoe High School. I met Jimmy L. Stanley, who was from Conetoe, about two years before I graduated from Conetoe High and married him my senior year. He was in service in the Korean Conflict about 1951. I did not go to college nor did I want to go to college. I decided I just wanted a job other than cleaning house after school.

Nursing Career

I went to work at Edgecombe General Hospital, when it was downtown, in June 1952, just to have a job, not to be a nurse. After I worked at Edgecombe General a while I became interested in becoming a nurse. At that time you could work eighteen months in a hospital, under a registered nurse, and take the state board exam and become an LPN waiver by examination. Yes, we took the test. In eighteen months, they were getting ready to close out that program at the time and one of the nurses said, "You know what Mrs. Stanley, I believe you can pass that test."

I said, "I will take it if you will sign for me." She did and I took the state board for an LPN and I passed.

After passing that I started working as an LPN by waiver of examination. Back then we had different caps from the LPN now. We had a little insignia that you put on your caps.

After I worked for two years or more, I decided to go to Wilson Hospital to work. I went there in 1965 and worked there until 1970. Wilson had a nursing school. While I was there, Wilson Technical School opened for LPNs and they said if you had taken the waiver of examination test, you could take the classes. If you took the classes and if you passed everything you could get waiver taken off your license. I took the classes and would you believe, I passed it by exam. I never had medical surgery, I never took OB/Gyn, I never took pediatrics. I passed all those tests but I felt within myself that I needed nutrition and diet therapy, and pharmacology, because I felt I did not know enough about medicine. I felt I needed one other thing, pediatrics. Those were the only education classes I took as an LPN. I took them and passed them and got waiver off my license.

The folks said go back for one more year and you can become an RN. Dr. Barb said to me, "Mrs. Stanley, I think we can get you some money to go to school."

I said, "I do not know how in the world I am going to college, with a son coming out of college and a daughter going in."

Dr. Barb's wife, Carolyn, said, "I will see what I can do." And she worked on a scholarship for me. I worried about that scholarship and finally I said, I know the Lord and I am not going to worry about that scholarship any more. I gave it to Him that day and the next week I got a scholarship. That scholarship paid for my uniform, everything. The only thing I had to pay was for insurance. My daughter was in school and so I went to school five days and worked Friday, Saturday, and Sunday at the hospital; therefore, I had enough money to send her some spending money, if she needed it.

So I went back one more year. I started in Wilson in 1968. My mother died in 1960 and daddy in 1968. My aunt was taking care of my sister Mamie, and after she died I had to place my sister in a nursing home. I came back home in 1970 and had my classes transferred to Edgecombe Community College and that is where I finished. I took state board in 1976 and became a registered nurse. I said I do not ever want to see another school.

Wesleyan College had a class, a trial thing for RNs, and I went there for two years, part time and worked as well. But their classes faded out. I started taking classes at East Carolina University. I got tired of that and started a regency program out of New York.

I had finished all of my education. The only thing I had to take was one test and go to New York for two weeks and I would have had my BSN. By that time I was getting ready to retire, I had been to school all of my life. I retired in 1995.

Married Life

We had been in Princeville since 1953. We bought a house that year and moved out from my parents'. I had just come home from the hospital when Hurricane Hazel came through. My son, Morris Lee Stanley, was a newborn baby and we were sitting by the window with all that wind coming through watching the wind. I had never seen a hurricane before and did not know the danger. But we got along fine.

We had bought an old house and it was well put together and sturdy and it did not do any damage to the house other than blow a few shingles off the roof. My husband went up on top of the house, while the eye of the storm was going through, and he was trying to fix a leak and did not know what a hurricane was or that the center of the storm, called the eye, was calm and it almost blew him off the roof.

Jimmy and Carrie Stanley bought this house in Princeville, North Carolina, in 1953. (Photo by Minniejo Gay.)

Both of my children are three years apart, both born October 1st. In 1958 when my daughter Felecia Stanley was a baby and we had a flood that year but the water only came up a ways. I could stand in the road and look at the water. It never came into my yard. I had to get shots for my daughter and that's how I remember. One other time we had a flood and it came into my neighbor's yard but our house is on a rise and it never came up that high. This was before the big dike was put up. After the dike was put up we never had anymore trouble with flooding until the big 500 Year Flood.

My son, Morris Lee, is 46 years old. He graduated from Wesleyan College. When I went to college to become an RN, he was a senior in college, coming out, and my daughter was a freshman going in college. My son took biology, and he is working at a pharmaceutical plant. He is in Fort Mill, South Carolina, at Leiner Health Products and is director of East Manufacturing. He was a plant manager in Iowa. They sold the plant. He has done very well and has traveled a lot.

His wife, Katherine Williams Stanley, is a school teacher and they have four children. The oldest, Krystal, is 21 years old, graduated from Iowa State University in three years. Her major is child psychology and Spanish. The next one, Kelly, is 14 and she is in high school and they has a son, Brett, ten years old. The youngest child, Skyler, is nine years old and she and Kelly are both in school.

My daughter, Felecia Williams, is a registered nurse. She went to A&T State University and is working at Wake Medical in the Cardiac Unit. She is day supervisor in charge of education. Her husband is Quentin Williams and he is Superintendent of Building for Carolina Power and Light Company in Raleigh and is working on his master in business administration.

I told my children my favorite quote, " Seek you first the kingdom of Heaven and all His righteousness, everything will be added unto you." My son has done that.

I remember when he was in high school and not half getting his lessons and I was so worried about him. My angel, the Lord, spoke to me and said, he's going to be alright. And I thought, he's going to be all right for school. But the Lord has wonderfully blessed him, he has traveled, he has had good jobs, he has a nice family, he has just done so well and I always tell him "Always put the Lord first." He was plant manager in a plant in Iowa. I worried about him because he wasn't around anybody but white people. I did not know how things were. They were so nice to him and did not want him to leave but they sold that plant to somebody else.

You will have friends tell you you ought to do this or that. But remember what your parents taught. My son said, "You set an example for us and I work hard to set an example for my children." He never talked back or argued and my daughter was a different personality. She was stubborn. But she is good to us. I tell her Jimmy and I are the children and she is the mama. She takes such good care of us. Felicia does not have any children but she looks out for her nieces and nephews.

So both of my children are doing real good.

The 500-Year Flood

That flood was probably the most frightened I have ever been. That night we stayed in the shelter because there was a tree and a telephone pole and with all that rain, if it had fallen it could crash right into our bed. We went to the shelter at Martin Middle School to spend the night. It rained

Jimmy and Carrie Stanley's home is shown during the "Flood of the Century." (Photo by Wayne Trevathan.)

more than I have ever seen, it came through the doors, all on the floors, and we got up the next morning and went home. We had no damage—just brushes against the house, so we decided to ride around to see what damage had been done to other people. While we were out I noticed one of my neighbors had water up to the fender of his truck . . . but he lived kind of down in a slope. Out by Shiloh . . . water, water, water. But the night before we left they told us, "We are going to have a flood so you need to get out." We went to MacMilliam Drive to a friend's house who lived on about a mile out. She said nobody told us about it. So we went back home and put all my clothes where I wouldn't have to look for them.

About twelve that night a neighbor knocked on the door and said, " Mr. Stanley, they say we got to get out." We got up and dressed again and went back to my friends house. I kept looking out the back because it is low out back. I told my husband, don't get anything . . . just come on. I was scared then and my mind said get your medicine, get all your medicine, and I did, but my husband did not get all his.

The next morning one of the fire/rescue persons came by and said, Mrs. Stanley, I passed by your house and you can't see nothing but the roof. And on the television the next morning I saw my house! My house is a tall, big old house, and it has a tall gable-end and that water was right up to that gable.

We stayed out there with my friend for almost three weeks. We looked everywhere for houses. There were no houses. My daughter came home and she kept telling us, you all come on and go home with me, so you can get a good bath. She lives in Apex. But we could not leave because there were lines everywhere. You had to get in line so you could get help. You had to get in line to pick up supplies for clothing, food, and then they started taking application for FEMA and we could not leave, so she came one day and she took her daddy to feed him and buy him some shoes and I stayed in line and then took me out to eat and bought me some shoes. We never went to her house, because there were lines for this and lines for that and everything. And you went through so much for FEMA. You had a number, always, and if you did not have that number, you could not get anything. You had to apply and one day I remember the people from Social Services were giving out some money and my husband and I went up there at five o'clock in the morning and when we got there some peoples were already there. That's how bad it was and I don't ever want to see another line. The Red Cross was feeding people and you had to get in line for that.

Nobody knows how horrible it was. Helicopters all over, bringing in food and water. You couldn't flush the bathroom, couldn't drink the water. You have to know what a blessing it was. God did not let me worry about anything. God will give you peace in a time of storms. I never worried about anything that I lost. I lost my piano and some of my pictures of my children, but I never . . . . Some people even lost the money they got from FEMA. Even though they were telling them constantly, don't let anybody do anything on your house. There were people coming in saying let me do this and that and they did not have license and they were telling people things. They did not wait on the Lord. I am just getting a house but I waited on the Lord. Seems like things are working out better because I did not push but left it up to him.

Her Motto

Well, my number one motto. 'Seek you first the Kingdom of God." That's what I want to tell my grandchildren. They are good children. You see, today, children that are so hyperactive. My grandchildren are not like that. You tell them to do something, they do it. You say, don't touch that, they do not touch it. They were like that when they were little.

I leave this wisdom to them and it is from experience: "Always put God first" and remember what your parents taught you.

Numerous floods have plagued Princeville over the centuries. (Courtesy of ECML.)

Andrew "Buck" Jackson Horne was a World War I veteran. (Courtesy of Mary Lewis Deans.)

Chapter Four
Veterans

Andrew "Buck " Jackson Horne was a World War I veteran and was born on November 13, 1894, and passed away on September 17, 1997. Interview by Mary Lewis Deans, November 5, 1996. Reprinted with the permission of Our State magazine from the November 1997 issue.

On the Saturday before Christmas Eve in 1917, I was over on Washington Street here in Rocky Mount, going north to a tailor shop to get my clothes, and a policeman stopped me. He knew me, and he called me by my name. He said, "Hey, Buck, come on here. I want to see you a minute. Why didn't you answer your call?"

I said, "What kind of call?"

He said, "You were supposed to go to the army."

I told him I didn't know anything about it, that I hadn't had any call to go to the army. I told him that I had all my papers from the local board at home. I said, "I haven't had a call."

He said, "I got to hold you for a slacker," and just like that, he locked me up.

The next morning came, and a man named Mr. King brought breakfast to the jail. I said, "Mr. King, I want you to do something for me this morning."

He said, "What is it?" I told him, "You know my daddy, Pompeii Horne. We live on 416 Woodland Avenue. I want you to go there this morning and tell my daddy to look in the bottom of my trunk and get all the mail I have in there from the local board and bring it to me."

Mr. King brought me the papers, and I put them in my coat pocket. At two o'clock the next morning, they handcuffed me to a policeman and put me on Train #82, the train that goes from Tampa to New York. We got off in Petersburg around daybreak, and we walked about one mile from the train station to Camp Lee. I was still handcuffed to that policeman.

When we got there, we went to headquarters. There were sergeants, lieutenants, captains, and colonels sitting around. I guess they were there for breakfast. We went to the office of the commander of the camp. This captain told us, "Come in. Come on in. Have a seat." He told the policeman to take the handcuffs off me.

The policeman took off the handcuffs and took out his papers and handed them to the captain. The captain looked at the papers and said to me, "Why didn't you answer your call?"

I said, "I haven't gotten any call. Then, I got the papers out of my pocket and said, "Here are all the papers I have gotten from the local board." He took my papers and looked at them. Then, he looked back at the papers the policeman had, and he kept on looking back and forth between papers. I said to myself right then, 'There is something wrong."

Finally, he looked at the policeman, and said, "Look here, policeman, I believe y'all brought the wrong man. You go on home. I am going to telegram back to the local board tomorrow, and, if this is the right man, we will send you the $50 bounty."

The captain looked at me and said, "You can go on back home if you want to, but you are going to be called in a few more days." Well, I decided to stay. I didn't do a thing but eat and sleep and play basketball for about 10 days. After 10 days, I was mustered in. (The North Carolina State Archives gives Mr. Horne's induction date as December 24,1917.)

After I was mustered into the army at Fort Lee, they sent me to Camp Upton at Newport News, Virginia. That was early in 1918. There they issued me army clothes and gear, and they sent the clothes I was wearing back home. I don't know how long I stayed there, maybe two months. Then, they shipped me to Bordeaux, France.

We left Newport News about 2:00 one afternoon, and we were 21 days going over to France. We had to zig-zag this way for a day or so, then zig-zag that way for a day or so, dodging mines and enemy submarines—the Kaiser's submarines. The Kaiser was the man then. Certain parts of the Atlantic Ocean were full of German submarines.

When we got to the English Channel, the navy had a submarine chaser and a torpedo boat to lead us. The submarine chaser circled all around us, just like a bird dog running around a bush. When he would catch the sound of a submarine, he would sound the alarm.

The morning we were crossing the channel, around 9:00, I was on the upper deck, getting ready to step down to go in for breakfast, and the submarine chaser sounded off. It was a mile out in front of us. A submarine came up behind us and shot out a torpedo. It missed us by about six feet. The submarine chaser dropped depth charges. I guess they dropped around 15 or 20 of them. They were just about the size of a big barrel. They got the submarine. We saw the oil coming up to the surface. Just as soon as we saw the oil, we knew they had the submarine.

In France, my job was to unload ammunition. I was in Company A, and we lived right beside the main train line. We took the ammunition off the train and loaded it on trucks for the front line. The Red Cross had a train—I reckon about 10 or 15 cars—that would go to the front line every morning and come back in the evening with the wounded. I could hear them hollering and moaning as they were taking them to the hospital.

I finally got promoted to corporal. With a truck, eight men, and a truck driver, my job was to put sand in the holes in a certain distance of the highway to the front. The big, American trucks knocked the road full of holes, so for eight or rune months I hauled sand to the holes.

The war was over when I had served my time out. It took us eight days and nights to cross the Atlantic. I was discharged in Petersburg (honorably discharged on July 8, 1919) and came home on Train #89, which got in Rocky Mount around 12:30. When I got home, my daddy was there for dinner; my mama was lying on the couch in the middle of the room, sick with the flu. There were a lot of folks sick with the flu.

Tarboro held a World War I welcome home celebration. (Courtesy of ECML.)

T.B. Wells was a veteran of World War II. His wife, Ruth G. Wells, is a retired school teacher. (Courtesy of Minniejo Gay.)

Theophilus Bryan Wells Jr. was born on September 30, 1911 and died August 14, 2000. His father was Theophilus Bryan Wells (1884–1946) and his mother was Minnie Price Wells. He had two sisters, Mary Bryan and Matilda. He married Grace Ruth Garrett on December 24, 1948. They raised three boys, Bryan Garrett, William Drake, and Stephen Moore Wells. Theophilus circled the world in his tour of duty with the U.S. Army in WWII. Interview by his wife, Ruth Garrett Wells.

Tour of Duty

On December 7, 1941, the day Pearl Harbor was bombed, I was sitting at home alone listening to music on the radio. I turned the radio off when the music was interrupted and then turned it back on, curious at what was going to happen, and I heard the news about the bombing at Pearl Harbor and President Roosevelt requested that Congress declare war on Japan as I listened to the radio.

There was a recruiting poster in the post office that showed Uncle Sam pointing his finger. Wherever you were, his eyes followed you.

I joined the military on November 19, 1942, Fort Bragg, North Carolina. While we were at Ft. Bragg they gave us tests such as aptitude, physical, and placement. We left Ft. Bragg December 3, 1942 and traveled to Keesler Field, Mississippi, and then on to Sioux Falls, South Dakota, arriving on Christmas Day in 1942. While in Sioux Falls, I received training for radio operator and mechanic and left South Dakota on May 19, 1943, and from there went to Boca Raton, Florida, and on to Goldsboro, North Carolina. While in Goldsboro I was finally able to see my family and friends for the first time since I had left home seven months before.

From Goldsboro I traveled to Camp Patrick Henry, Virginia to get on the *H.M.S. Andes*, which was a British ship. We arrived in Camp Don B. Passage, Casablanca, North Africa, on December 15, 1943. While in Casablanca there was more training for conditioning to war.

We left North Africa on January 17, 1943, by a train. They said it was a 40 + 8 train, which means that there was only enough room for forty men and eight horses. We arrived in Bombay, India on the *H.M.S. Chantilly*, only to leave to travel to Calcutta on May 28, 1944. We never knew where we were going. We relied on something called the "Shit House Rumor" to have some knowledge on where the next stop would be.

We arrived in Kunming, China, on April 7, 1944, and received assignment to 21st Photo Rec. Sqdn. APO 627.

Most Americans have always been traditionally religious, especially during wartime, and church services were provided on base. While I was in China, I visited in the home of missionaries that were serving there. There was also "Fox Hole" religion, which was a term relating to rough and scary times.

T.B. Wells was photographed in Kumming, China, during WWII. (Courtesy of Minniejo Gay.)

For the Service men there were U.S.O. shows and I remember one show that had Pat O'Brien as a guest.

Being in the remote area of China, the news we received there was sketchy. I didn't know of the invasion of the Allies on D-Day, having learned about what happened later. War is Hell. The invasion of D-Day was probably necessary, but it remains a tragedy. That decision to drop the Atomic bomb on Japan was critical to end the war, but a tragic loss of innocent lives. Americans, at the time of the bombing, were so relieved that the war was over that they didn't take it into account what had really happened in Hiroshima. It was years later that the Americans saw Hiroshima and Nagasaki as real places with human beings who paid a price for someone else's decision.

The Home Front

We wrote letters but could not reveal any information regarding location or destination. Any such information would be blacked out by a black pen. Being the only male member of age in the family, I was the only one to serve in the war, but Mother and my sisters helped me through the war with letters from home. Letters from the family sometimes came several letters at once and I put them in order by date. I wanted to know any news about my father's condition as he had suffered a stroke shortly before I went into the military.

V-Mail was something only used by the military people who had a special machine that could reduce the size of the letter and in doing that it reduced the bulk of the mail in general. Military personnel didn't have to use stamps, only write FREE where a stamp would normally be.

Letters from home told of the sacrifices made by the Americans remaining there. Gas, sugar, shoes, and tires were only a few of the items that were rationed during wartime. Stickers were used for gas; an "A" sticker meant gas allotted for pleasure driving and a "B" sticker could mean more gas for business purposes. My family always had a garden, but other Americans put a lot of effort into their own gardens to help with shortages.

Back home scrap metal and scrap rubber drives, as well as War Bond drives, were held. Places were designated in town to collect the scrap metal and scrap rubber in areas that were convenient to patrons. At the movies the newsreels showed advertisements on buying of War Bonds and movie stars promoted this.

With the shortages there were Rationing Boards, where members of the community served and interviewed to determine the amount of food and other necessities that were needed. Sugar was one item that was needed for canning and gasoline needed to transport members of the family to the doctor.

The Eastern Coast of America was in danger during the war but I had every faith in the American Soldiers to win the war. We had blackouts at the beach, cars not traveling at night with lights on, and many people had black curtains on their windows.

The incarcerating of Japanese Americans was the correct move at the time. Americans could not trust any Japanese after the bombing of Pearl Harbor and it was for their protection.

Pa said that Americans could sympathize with those who lost homes and jobs and the many families that were separated; however, it would have never happened without a war.

As to the role women took in the war, women replaced men in factories. They also helped with management of farms in the absence of men.

Most families had the blue and gold star flags and one hung in my home that showed there was one family member serving in the military.

Homer Parham Braswell Jr. was a friend of T.B. Wells. (Courtesy of Minniejo Gay.)

Homer P. Braswell

As in any war there is a tragic side. Many people were killed and wounded senselessly. My best friend and a native of Whitakers is an example. Homer P. Braswell was the kind of guy that anybody would love. Homer was a pilot in the U.S. Air Force and was captured after the fall of Bataan by the Japanese. He was a part of the Death March, I learned later. I found out that the Death March was something that the Japanese did to the American Soldiers that were captured. The Japs starved the Americans and made them walk day and night, in any weather condition, until they dropped dead, hence the name Death March. But Homer survived this and was later killed on a Japanese ship carrying prisoners to Japan. This ship was torpedoed by American Forces, not knowing that there were American Soldiers on board. I got news of his death in a letter from Mother.

Feelings about the War

Adolf Hitler of Germany, Benito Mussolini of Italy, and Hedeki Tojo of Japan were ruthless, greedy, and heartless men. The German concentration camps were the ugliest faces of this horrible war. The cruel destruction of millions of Jews as the result of the sick mind of Hitler is a reality Americans must never forget.

This was a war of the common soldier as well as military leaders. Dwight D. Eisenhower was a very capable, outstanding leader. George Patton was one of the greatest military leaders ever. Douglas MacArthur said, "I shall return," but he was removed from position of leadership because of insubordination. Omar Bradley was the advisor and commander of ground forces in Europe. He will be remembered, in my mind, as essential in decisions.

The 50th Anniversary of the events of World War II has passed and I do not know of all the things that are being done about it. But I am pleased that I had the opportunity to share my experiences and opinions and they will be passed on to the next generation. As the years pass and my generation, who participated in the war, are no longer living, the war must be kept alive through our grandchildren. The history of war is best recorded by those who were in the war. I pray my children and children's children will never be called upon to pay the price of experiencing war again.

Milton Alvin Moore Jr. is an avid naturalist and outdoorsman. (Photo by Bill Goode.)

Chapter Five
Tarboreans

Milton Alvin Moore Jr. was born in the county seat of Tarboro, where he still lives, on July 24, 1928. His father was Milton Alvin Moore Sr. and his mother was Dixie Lee Rodwell. His maternal grandparents were Edmund Thomas Rodwell (1860–1935) and Leila Drake (1882–1974). He is a retired pharmacist. Interview by Traci Thompson, January 9, 2002.

My name is M.A. Moore Jr. I was born and raised in Tarboro. My father came to Tarboro in 1924 after his graduation from the pharmacy school at the University of North Carolina. He worked for a drugstore named McNair & Bryan. After that, he went to work for R.E.L. Cook & Company. In 1941, my mother purchased R.E.L. Cook & Company and we renamed it Moore's Pharmacy. After attending the public schools in Tarboro, I went to Fishburne Military School in Virginia, graduated from there in 1946, and attended pharmacy school at the University of North Carolina beginning in 1946 and graduating in 1951. I graduated in June, took the state board in June and passed it, came home and entered into the practice of pharmacy in Tarboro, and I practiced in Edgecombe County for 45 years.

Family

The earliest person that I know of in my family was a man named Garret Van Zandt, who came from the city of Tread in Holland to America in 1646.

My grandmother's father was a man named Drake who could trace his ancestry back to Sir Francis Drake. Her mother's name was Van Zandt; her mother's father was a man named McKeon who was a physician and a professor of medicine at Edinburgh University in Scotland.

Joseph L. Rodwell was my great-great-great-great grandfather. He came from Yorkshire in England in 1740 and ultimately settled in Warren County, North Carolina. My mother was from Warren County, even though she was born in Florala, Alabama.

My grandfather lived on the family land up in Warren County. He became quite knowledgeable in the logging and lumber industries. He went to work for a hardware corporation based in Louisville, Kentucky. He worked his way up to the point where he was the southern regional manager and went to Florala, Alabama. There was an offshoot of the Rodwell family there, a cousin who was in the mercantile business. After a few years, granddaddy got lonesome for Warren County. He went to Warrenton and opened a hardware business called Rodwell Brothers Hardware.

My grandfather, Edmund Thomas Rodwell, was one of the most well-thought of people in the town of Warrenton. During the Depression, people would go to him, and he would lend them money to keep people from starving. He would give a man enough fertilizer, seed, and tools to make another crop. And 90-some-odd percent of those loans were repaid.

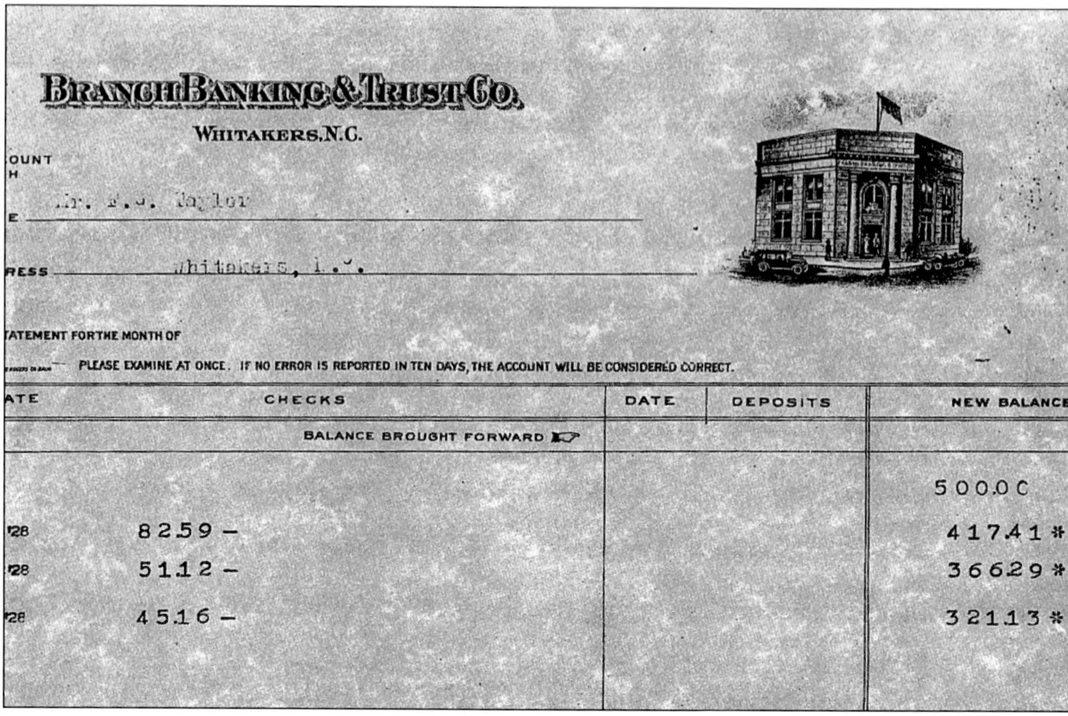
BRANCH BANKING & TRUST CO.
WHITAKERS, N.C.

OUNT
H
E Mr. F. J. Taylor
RESS Whitakers, N. C.

TATEMENT FOR THE MONTH OF

PLEASE EXAMINE AT ONCE. IF NO ERROR IS REPORTED IN TEN DAYS, THE ACCOUNT WILL BE CONSIDERED CORRECT.

ATE	CHECKS	DATE	DEPOSITS	NEW BALANCE
	BALANCE BROUGHT FORWARD			
				500.00
'28	82.59 –			417.41 *
'28	51.12 –			366.29 *
'28	45.16 –			321.13 *

This 1929 bank statement was issued just before the Great Depression. (Property of Pete Taylor.)

In 1947, I had to go to Warrenton for a funeral. I went downtown. There were a lot of people who were kin to me, and I always see someone I know. A man walked up to me, looked like he was 90 years old. He said, "Aren't you Mr. Ed Rodwell's grandson?" I said, "Yes, sir." He said, "Well, in 1930, he loaned me $300 dollars, and he kept my family from starving. I never have paid that money back, and it's been on my conscience. He's been dead since 1935, and it's been on my conscience ever since. I want to pay it back, and pay the interest that would have accrued with it. If you go to the bank with me, we'll figure up exactly what I owe you as of right now." I said, "Well you don't owe it to me, you owe it to my grandmother." So the banker figured and gave me a check for several times more than $300.

I came home, and my grandmother was sitting in the living room reading. She hadn't felt like going to the funeral. I told her about the man paying the money back, and I handed her the check. She said, "Give me your pen." I thought she was going tell me to deposit it for her, or cash it. She said, "Here, put that in your education account." I always cry when I talk about my grandmother and granddaddy. I loved them; God knows I loved them.

Early Childhood

I was born in Tarboro in 1928. We lived here for awhile, and when I was three, my father and another man bought a drugstore over in Roxboro, North Carolina, and we moved to Roxboro. I remember the day we moved, and where I stood. I remember being sad. The house is still standing, right up the street here. I lived in Roxboro for about a year and a half. My daddy was about to lose the drugstore; he opened a business at the very wrong time, right at the first of the Depression. My grandfather came up there and he didn't particularly like the way we were living. He just told my mother, "You can come to Warrenton if you want to. If you don't you can stay here, but this boy is going with me." I was three. I went to live with my grandfather for almost five years, and he'd bring me to Tarboro every once in awhile.

Rodwell Brothers Hardware was a huge influence on my life. I spent hours in that hardware store, down in the blacksmith shop, where there was a black man I called Uncle John. He could do anything in the world with iron and wood. He used to make wagons, buggies. He used to make me little swords that were real sharp. My grandmother would find them and take them down to the basement and grid the edge off on an emery wheel.

After daddy lost his drugstore, he came back to Tarboro. That's when he went to work for Mr. Cook. My daddy was a brilliant pharmacist, but he wasn't a businessman. My mother owned the store; she was the business person.

Tarboro was home. My granddaddy died, and I came back here. That was the year that I went to the first grade in school. By that time things were more promising money-wise for the family, and my grandmother came to live with us. My grandmother had the greatest influence upon me of any person in my life. Every day was a lesson. You should do this, and you should not do that. You're going to be a gentleman, or I'm going to die trying! I think she was successful.

Childhood Mischief

Here's a story of youthful mischief, one for which I got a terrific licking. In front of my grandmother's front porch there was a row of bushes with little white bell-shaped flowers on them, and they were just loaded with bumblebees. I was forever catching them. On the day of the incident, I had been out there early—it was in the summertime—and caught a mayonnaise jar half full of great ol' big black bumblebees. Well, that day my grandmother was having the garden club meeting. The house had a fairly large entrance hall, and on the right was the living room. There was a bunch of women in there, and on the left was the dining room, and the dining room table was covered with good little things to eat, like ham biscuits made with a beaten biscuit, not a store-bought biscuit, but a *hard* beaten biscuit. Little cucumber sandwiches, and 15 or 20 other good things to eat. I don't know what flew into me. I always said later that the devil made me do it, but I went in the middle of that hall and set that jar full of bumblebees down and took the lid off. Well, in a few minutes, that broke up the garden club meeting! Women were running out of the house everywhere. I knew I had better make my escape. When my grandmother ran out on the front porch, I ran up the back stairs. She had a sewing room that went off of the second floor landing. There was a huge dormer that went out there. I went out that dormer window and went around and got between one of the chimneys and the house. She knew I'd hid up there, and she walked out in the yard and said, "I know where you are, and you can stay up there until it gets dark, but I'm going to catch you sometime, and I'm going to give you a whipping you're not going to forget!" Well, I sat up there and sat up there. There were two ways down. If you weren't scared, you could go down and the front porch kind of went down at a slant. It was a right good drop, I'd say at least 14 feet, but I'd jump off of it. It was a wonder I didn't break my neck; but I'd done it before, so I jumped off. I'd no more than hit the ground good and was trying to get myself together to stand up and she had me. She carried me in the house, and she did give me a whipping sure enough!

I was telling my granddaddy the story—he'd gotten home about 15 minutes after she'd whipped me, and he didn't like for me to be whipped. He said, "There are other ways." He would fuss with her when she'd whip me. I was sitting in his lap telling him the story, and he was doing his best to keep from grinning. Talk about a wonderful man!

I messed with bees so much that in the long run, I got stung real bad one day and I started swelling up. My grandmother, who I called mama, grabbed me up and threw me in the car and we went to Dr. Pete's office. She carried me in there, he took one look at me, and my grandmother said, "Bees." So he grabbed the syringe and started sticking a couple of things in my arm, laid me on the table, and a nurse he had held an oxygen mask over my nose. After awhile I started feeling better, and I told her I could breathe all right, and she took that off. He came in there and took my pulse, listened to my heart, and decided to pronounce me alive.

I had an accident with a firecracker. Right across the railroad down on Albemarle Avenue, on Main Street side—that's two blocks off of Main Street, west—right in front of the water plant on the other side of the street, the town used to keep telephone poles. They kept big piles of stoker coal, too, that was used in the power plant, which was sort of across the street too. And we used to go over there and sit and play on those telephone poles. It was around Christmas. Back then, I think it was for something like $14.95, you could send a money order for that amount to a firecracker company. We'd always buy what was called the Young American Firecracker Assortment. It was a bunch of firecrackers. Some of everything there was. The only way they could ship it was by the railroad. It came in a wood box by about 5 feet long, 14 or 15 inches wide, and about 10 inches deep. And it was ram-crammed with firecrackers. We'd save our money all year to get one.

I had a pocket full of three-inch firecrackers, and we were over there one afternoon after school right around Christmas. There were a bunch of us shooting off firecrackers. We'd light them with a thing called "punk," a stick that would smolder. I had just lit a three-inch firecracker and somebody threw one under my feet, and I forgot the one in my hand for a brief second and it exploded in my hand. And it hurt like hell. I opened my hand and looked. And when a firecracker explodes in your hand, it's sort of silvery black looking. It burned so bad, there was a mudhole down there full of filthy water, but I crammed my hand right down in that cold water. I pulled out my pocket handkerchief and crammed it in there and soaked it and put it in the palm of my hand and jumped on my bicycle and rode two or three blocks down to Dr. Bass' office.

Walked right in the front door. The waiting room was to the left, front door opened into a long hall that went the length of the building. I didn't even go in the waiting room; I went right straight back there by Doc's office and there was a sink. I never will forget it, because you had to work the controls with your elbows. I turned that cold water on, I was standing there holding that hand under there, well Doc hadn't been busy when I went in there and he saw me. He came out there and took a hold of my hand and looked at it and said, "Firecracker?" I said, "Yes, sir." He said, "You're lucky you ain't lost a finger." So he put a big pad of tannic acid gauze—that's what they put on burns then—on there and kind of wrapped it up a little bit. He said, "You know when you get home, the first thing your grandmother is going to say is 'What happened to your hand,' don't you?" I said, "Yes, sir." He said, "What are you going to say?" I said, "I'll make up something!"

I did that many a time. I'd hurt something. I wouldn't let anybody know. I'd go right straight to Dr. Bass. I had a Benjamin pump-up air pistol that shot BBs. Wasn't a thing in the world but an air pump and a cylinder. I was pumping that thing up one day and it had a BB in it. It had leaked down. I pumped, pumped, pumped—and damn if the trigger didn't go off. I've got a BB right inside my leg, right there right now. I said, "You damn fool, sit here and shoot yourself." And I was up here where I lived then, in front of Martin Middle School. I said, "Hell, he ain't going to get that out of there I know, but I'd better go." I went down to the doctor's office. He said, "What's wrong?" I told him what happened. He said, "Well, drop your pants." Neat little hole right there, copper-plated BB. And he felt around, and said, "Yeah, I found it, but it's deep. Do more harm trying to get it out." I said, "Well, leave it in." It's still in there. What your body will do is just encapsulate it.

Military School and Beyond

An interesting story that occurred while I was at Fishburne: I was Corporal of the Guard one day. It was April 12, 1945. The commandant walked into the office, the guardroom. I stood up and reported to him as we were supposed to do, and he said "Corporal Moore, lower the flag to half mast. The President is dead." Kind of took me by surprise; I was shocked. And I said, "Sir?" and he repeated it. So a Private of the Guard, and I climbed to the highest point at Fishburne Military School at the tower where the flagpole was and lowered the flag to half-mast. After the flag was lowered, I walked over to one of the crenelations in the battlement at the top of that tower, and stood staring out over the town of Waynesboro, down into the valley of the Wayne River, and the thought that went

Milton Alvin Moore Jr. attended Fishburne Military School in 1946. (Courtesy of M.A. Moore Jr.)

through my mind was, what will this country do now? Franklin Roosevelt was a tremendously great president. He had the capability to mobilize the country to do way beyond what it had ever done. To help England, and to defeat Adolf Hitler, and the Emperor of Japan. But neither one of those two evil men reckoned upon the might and the motivation of the American people.

Born here, practically raised here, I have never, ever been away from here for more than a week at a time that I didn't get homesick, homesick to the point that it was almost to be considered a disease. The first year I went to Fishburne Military School, in the spring, I didn't think I could stand it. I came home for Christmas and my daddy said I'd better stand it. It was in the early spring, and in the afternoon after drill, I'd be sitting up there in my room on the second floor and the drill field was literally covered with robins. And that chirp, chirp, chirp . . . and I got to thinking about my buddies at home, fishing for rock [striped bass], fishing for shad. And I really got bad off. So I just walked right down, made sure I was neat and orderly, and I went right over to the superintendent's office, Colonel Hudgens. Asked for permission to speak to him. Went in there, took myself in there to one step in front of his desk, stood at attention, saluted him, and asked permission to talk to him.

He says, "Certainly. Have a seat."

And I told him, I said, "Colonel, if I don't go home for a little bit I'm going to die."

He said, "What's wrong?"

I said, "I'm so homesick I can't stand it, and those damn robins out there, they just keep reminding me of what's going on at home."

He said, "Well. . . . " He looked at me. I knew him pretty well, because Colonel Hudgens taught me trigonometry, one on one. He said, "Well, I'll tell you what, Mr. Moore. When do you want to go?"

I said, "Right now." It was about 3:00 in the afternoon.

He said, "Well, I believe there's a bus that leaves for Charlottesville at 4:15. Can you make it?" I said, "Yes, sir! I'll be there."

I rode the bus to Richmond and made the bus driver stop at Broad Street station and let me off. I went over there to the Coastline Railroad station and asked, "What time is the next train?" There was a train leaving shortly going to Rocky Mount. So I bought a ticket and got on that. Got off at the station over here at Rocky Mount. It was in the early morning hours, about 3:00. I said, "How in the hell am I going to get home?"

Well, I was standing there pondering that, and a highway patrolman pulled up right beside me. He knew me. He said, "Sonny, what the hell are you doing standing out here on the street in Rocky Mount at 3:00 in the morning?" I told him I was trying to get home. He lived over here in Tarboro. He had to come over here to investigate a wreck that had occurred just across the railroad in Edgecombe County.

He carried me home, and I took my key and went in the house, and nobody heard me. I went in my room, shut the door, crawled in bed, and went to sleep. About 9:30 the next morning I woke up and opened the door and stepped out and my grandmother was right there in the hall and she liked to have fainted. She didn't know I was coming home. I never will forget that.

If you are born and raised in Tarboro, you can't help but love it. It's just something in your blood. You can't leave it for long. A week I can handle, but not much over. Tarboro is a unique place.

When I graduated from Fishburne in 1945, in August of that year is when Harry Truman saved me, when he dropped the atomic bomb. Had that not happened, almost surely I would have been in World War II; and had that not happened, there's no telling how many thousands of lives would have been lost in trying to invade the island of Japan.

I was, however, called to service on active duty in 1953, which was the tail end of the Korean War. I didn't have to go to Korea; I never went out of the country. I served half of my two year's time in Valley Forge Army Hospital and the other half in the main infirmary of the 82nd Airborne Division. I was a licensed pharmacist when that happened. I was the number one pharmacist of the 82nd Airborne Division infirmary. That didn't mean a whole lot; I just had another one working under me.

I was in the North Carolina National Guard for several years. I was in Company F, which is an infantry company, right here in Tarboro, and then when I got my license to practice pharmacy I was transferred to the medical company in Wilson.

TARBOREANS

My babysitter when I was a baby lived up the street here a ways, not two blocks from the library. Her name was Mrs. Maude Bynum. House on the corner up there, old gingerbread house, probably built about 1890 or 1895. Mrs. Maude Bynum was the mother of Lizzie Morrisette. Mr. Morrisette was the freight agent here for the Atlantic Coast Line Railroad. Lizzie Morrisette was the mother of Elizabeth Morrisette, nicknamed "Woody," who was my mother's closest friend, like an aunt to me; one of the sweetest women who ever lived. Right up in the next block from Miss Maude Bynum's house was her daughter, Lizzie Bynum Morrisette. The upstairs of that house was rented by my mother and father and that's where I was born. It was so hot, Dr. Bass who delivered me told me later—Dr. Bass being my best friend from the time I was born until he died at the age of 94—Dr. Bass said, "Sonny, it was so hot that day that the popcorn popped in the field." Until I was about six or seven years old I believed that.

Mrs. Maude Bynum used to babysit me, and she was stone deaf. Her best friend was a woman named Mrs. Katie Oats, who lived right down here in the house on the westerly corner of Park Avenue and Main. Mrs. Katie was deaf, too. But she and Mrs. Maude would sit there where they could look at each other and you'd see their lips moving but you wouldn't hear a sound, but they were having a conversation, because they could read each other's lips. They quite often were engaged in playing double solitaire with the first oval-shaped playing cards I ever saw.

Mrs. Maude had an old-fashioned speaking trumpet. She claimed to be deaf, but damn if she couldn't hear the telephone ring. She could speak, and she'd say, "Sonny," and I'd say "Yes, ma'am?" "Go answer the telephone." I used to wonder how in the hell could she not hear anything but she could hear that phone ring! The telephone was in the dining room, and I'd go back there and answer the telephone. Of course, Mrs. Maude couldn't talk on the phone, she had to go through somebody that could talk. But a lot of times it would be just, "Tell Mrs. Maude this," and I'd go back out there, and she had this speaking trumpet and she'd put it up to her ear and I'd tell her what the message was.

I never will forget, I spent many a night being babysat in Mrs. Maude's house, either by her or by Lizzie. After Lizzie's husband died, Lizzie moved in with her mother. Woody Morrisette married Manly Meredith Carstarphen. Manly and Woody were just like my aunt and uncle. I can remember Woody rocking me to sleep many a night when I was a baby. I loved her just like she was kin to me. I quite often visit her grave and my mother and father's grave in Greenwood Cemetery. I try to keep her grave just as neat and nice as I keep my mother and father's. She was a beautiful woman. She worked for "Dinksie" Gilliam, Don Gilliam Jr., who was clerk of the superior court. Woody worked for him for years. She died of lung cancer. They were wonderful people.

Another story I want to tell about Tarboro is the event that ultimately caused the law that prevents the sale of various kinds of fireworks in the state of North Carolina. The event that caused that law to be passed happened right downtown here. Downtown right now is Simmons Furniture Company, been there for over a hundred years, now run by a grandson of the founder, Jim Simmons Jr. Jim Simmons III, probably. Mr. Jim used to have these big tables out there in front of his store full of firecrackers and he sold a lot of them. Right across the street there was a man named Paul Shirley who also ran a grocery store over there. Paul had big tables full of firecrackers. I imagine there was over a ton of fireworks on display, anything you ever heard of.

Well, I'd been out at Shiloh Farms squirrel hunting. I was coming back into town driving an old '38 Chevrolet two-door sedan that my grandmother bought direct from the factory. I don't remember the exact year that this happened. But I was in about the middle of the town bridge across the Tar River when all hell broke loose. It looked like a war up there! There were skyrockets, Roman candles, two-shot repeaters, three-shot repeaters, every firework you can imagine was exploding in the middle of Main Street. It was something. I had my foot locked on the brake until I choked the engine down when I let out on the clutch. I was astounded. I said, "What in the hell is going on?" and then I realized exactly what was happening.

They say it began because somebody who was drunk bought a two-shot repeater over there on Paul Shirley's side of the street, set it off right next to the building, right up to the side of the building, and it went up and hit an overhanging ledge, fell back down into Shirley's firecrackers. They ignited and sent some across the street, which ignited Mr. Jim Simmons'.

I finally pulled up there, got me a parking place a little closer and walked up there. It was utter chaos. People screaming, hollering for help. I walked over there on Mr. Jim's side and there was a boy named Rufus Cromity who lived here. Mr. Jim's big plate glass window had shattered, and a triangular piece of that glass had gone right into Rufus' back. He had to be carried to the hospital. I don't remember exactly how bad it was. It didn't kill him—he became a Presbyterian preacher.

Right after that, they got together and passed the law and no more fireworks were sold in North Carolina. Not any that explode, go up in the air, and do a dozen other things.

There was a man named Tom Graham—not a man, but I reckon he was 18 or 19 years old—he lived right next door to us. He wasn't exactly right. He was strong as a bull, and he was so frightened by the fireworks that he wedged himself in between the curb and the side of an automobile and lifted the automobile up enough to crawl under it. A fellow told me he saw him do it. This same individual,

DAILY SOUTHERNER

WANT TO SELL? WANT TO BUY? TRY A WANT AD

Tarboro, North Carolina, Thursday, December 26, 1946 — Full Associated Press Wi

Fireworks Explosion Damages Downtown Area

This headline appeared in the Daily Southerner *on December 26, 1946.*

Tom Graham, in later days—I reckon he was probably in his 30s—was getting worse and worse. He was a schizophrenic. He told me one day that they were watching him. I said, "What do you mean, they're watching you?" He said, "They've got our house wired. They've got little things that can see me, and they listen to everything I do and when I come outdoors they've got cameras and they're watching everything I do. It's about to drive me crazy." And it did drive him crazy, because he took a .22 rifle and walked right out in the middle of the street in front of his house. I heard the gun go off; he shot himself, killed himself with a .22 rifle. I wanted to go out there but my grandmother had seen and put together what had happened. He had a brother named Ottie—Oswald Graham. This man's father was a veterinarian, and he had a brother who became a veterinarian just like his father had been.

One afternoon in the '40s, my friend Fred Hill and I had been messing around somewhere. He lived right over from the library here, in one of those houses on this side of Trade Street, and I pulled up there to let him out. All of a sudden we heard the damndest explosion, loud noise you've ever heard around here. I said, "What in the hell was that?" I said, "It sounds to me like the oil mill blew up!" Well, the oil mill was straight up the railroad and off to the left, out where Anaconda Road goes now. What it was was a steam engine, and the water had got below the plate in the boiler, and it was just like sealing up water and heating it – damn, something's got to give if you put all that steam in there. And it blew up. It killed two or three men. Blew the roof of the locomotive forward toward Rocky Mount. And there were brains all over it. I remember that. The track, the crossties, were shattered, and the rails had gone out from under the engine. The engine was a wreck. We went up to what we thought was the oil mill and we saw somebody just flying going out further—that was a dirt road then—and we went out there and we saw it. But it was a tremendous noise and it killed several people. Big headlines in all the Eastern papers about the Atlantic Coast Line engine blowing up.

PHARMACY

After my family purchased the drugstore, and I was the only child, my course of study was more or less set. After I graduated from the university and pharmacy school, I came back to Tarboro and that's where I worked until 1976. Then so many of these chain stores came in here. Customers would come in and tell you that they'd been to a chain, and gotten a quote on a prescription, and I couldn't buy it for anywhere near that, and I could see the handwriting on the wall. So, while I had something to sell I sold it, and went to work for somebody else, and let them worry about paying the bills; all they had to do was pay me a salary. The last place I worked, Dr. Lawrence Cutchin, a friend of mine, owned a little drugstore up in Whitakers. He asked me to go up there and run it. He said, "You ain't even got to worry about making money. I'd like to see you break even if possible, but I want my town to have a drugstore." And that's where I went; that's where I was working when a severe ailment of my spine caused me to have a big operation in December of 1989 and I haven't worked a day since.

Being a small-town country pharmacist in those days was a pleasure. I'd say that 50% of the people that got sick went to see the pharmacist before they went to the doctor, because they didn't have enough money to pay the doctor. And they could come talk to me for nothing. People appreciated what you did for them, then. A lot of our customers were rural people, farmers, black and white. They'd come in there and talk to Daddy when they were sick. My daddy, if he thought the person needed to see the doctor, he didn't make any bones about it; he would send them to a doctor. A lot of times the remedies were such that a pharmacist could treat the patient. When I got my license and went in there to really practice pharmacy, he told me and my mother, "No child will go out of this drugstore without the medicine they need, whether the parents or the person that brings them in has enough money to get it or not. No child is going to be denied medicine."

Back in the '40s there was a strike here at Hart Cotton Mill. We had a lot of customers that lived

Many drugstores have operated in Tarboro. (Courtesy of ECML.)

over there and didn't have any pay coming in. I remember Daddy telling a man, "Don't worry about your medicine; we'll take care of that. As long as I can get it, you can get it. If it gets to the point where we can't get it, we might have to try something, but that strike's not going to last forever. "

When I started practicing pharmacy, 50% of the medicine that was prescribed by doctors around here you had to make. You didn't pour it out of a bottle or count them out of a bottle; you had to make it from scratch. In your senior year of pharmacy school then, your main course was what was known as dispensing pharmacy. It was taught by a man named Ira Winfield Rose, a wonderful man, and a wonderful teacher. He was from Rocky Mount. He founded a drugstore named I.W. Rose Drug Company, and it was the first drugstore in Eastern North Carolina to gross over a million dollars a year. Dr. Rose and I were real close. He taught us all those things that you had to make. He said, "You don't just make them, you create them, because this is a skill, it's an art."

We learned how to properly fill capsules. We used the apothecary system of grains and drams and the pharmaceutical ounce. We had to learn how to make what is known as charts. A chart is a Latin word for "powder," just like a B.C. powder. You have to mix the ingredients, form them into a square or some way that you can divide evenly by a number. You mixed your powder on a pharmaceutical pill tile. It was a square twelve inches of glazed material.

You'd divide off your powders—you'd need two spatulas really to make powders correctly. You take your powder papers and fold one end up—a powder paper is about three inches, two and a half inches by three and a half. You'd fold up one of the long sides about an inch, and you would count out your papers and fold them correctly, and then you would take your spatula and if you had to make 36 charts you would remove 1/36th and put in the paper. Then you would fold them and, in the end, if you've ever seen a B.C. powder or a Stanback powder, that's what they're supposed to look like. Well, having folded I reckon ten thousand of them before I went to pharmacy school, my daddy having taught me how to do that when I was about ten or twelve years old, Dr. Rose used to say, "If y'all ever learn to fold powders as good as Mr. Moore can, you will be all right." He said, "He can fold them as fast as the machine over at the B.C. factory."

Then we had to make preparations like suppositories. Now, they have molds that you make them in. Drugstores advertise that they've got a compounding room, a little glassed off area. Hell, we didn't have no damn compounding room, we just put the pill tile or whatever we were going to work with down on one side of the prescription counter and get at it! We always used a highly accurate set of what an ordinary human being would think of as a pair of scales; they are actually called balances. They would weigh a pencil mark. We would weigh out ingredients. If I was making a suppository, I use one of the waxy-like substances that would absorb through the mucus membranes.

Let me give you the formula for a pile ointment that was known as North Carolina pile ointment. It contained, I believe, four grains of cocaine hydrochloride. It contained ten grains of menthol and ten grains of camphor, and ten drops of liquefied phenol. Phenol is carbolic acid. The way to make it is, you'd weigh all your ingredients. You'd have your carbolic acid in a medicine dropper or a pipette. It wouldn't be written, "ten drops," it would be written, "ten minims." A minim is the equivalent of a drop in most substances.

First you'd take the camphor and the menthol and put them there and mix them together, and bless Pat, when you mix camphor and menthol, they dissolve into a liquid. It's called a eutectic mixture. Then you would add the cocaine hydrochloride, work it around with your spatula. The cocaine would immediately dissolve in that little bit of liquid. Then you would add your phenol and then you would take an ounce of zinc oxide ointment, and you would incorporate the liquids into the ounce of the ointment which is a very stiff thing. And you would mix well by mashing down with the spatula. Pharmacists had spatulas, everything from a foot long right on down to two inches. You would mix it very well, because you didn't want all the active ingredients, for instance, four grains of cocaine hydrochloride, in one application. You're liable to knock the patient out. That was a common thing to make.

I've made ointments by the pound. In pharmacy school, you were taught to make such esoteric things as something that would resemble Pond's cold cream, or even harder, Pond's vanishing cream. Where you use waxes and substances that you have to heat in a water bath, if you don't know exactly what you're doing, you'll have a flop. Every pharmacy student used to keep an 8-ounce jar of Pond's cold cream and Pond's vanishing cream hidden in his little dispensing unit. For the same reason, we kept a bottle of bromo-seltzer, which is an effervescent powder. Effervescent powder is extremely hard to make. Of course, we'd all try. Had to, because the man was walking around looking at you. Not only Dr. Rose, but a lab assistant too. But if it didn't work, wouldn't go together, we always had that back-up, you know.

Farming

I used to like to get up and go to work, because I like people. I like country people, farming people. But I really didn't want to be a pharmacist. I wanted to be a forester or a farmer. But then, the only son of a family who owned a drugstore, my course in life was set. I wound up being lucky enough to farm for awhile, but it got to a point where I got out of farming because it was beginning to be unprofitable.

I was fortunate to become almost a member of a prominent farming family here in Edgecombe County. That was the Satterthwaite family. Mr. and Mrs. Jim Satterthwaite were the parents, and they had five children, all of them big, strapping boys. All those boys became my close friends, but one of them was the closest thing to a brother that I ever had. He was Josh Satterthwaite. Josh died on July 4, 1974. I never will forget it. I felt like half of me was gone. I miss him just about every day. He and I were so close. He was never married, and he and I did everything together. He taught me about everything there was to know then about farming. He and his father and his brother Jim, and his

Before tractors, plowing was done with a four-horse plow pulled by a mule. (Courtesy of ECML.)

brother Sam Satterthwaite who's still living, Powell, and J.R. . . . I was like a member of the family. As a matter of fact, before I got married, Mrs. Lil Satterthwaite had a sister that lived in that house out there near Coakley. She died, and Mr. Jim said, "Well, Doc"—that's what he called me—he said, "Why don't you put your clothes in that front room up there?" And I did. I'd come home sometimes from Chapel Hill on the weekend, and I'd go by the drugstore and say "Hey" and then go right out to Coakley and change clothes and say, "What y'all want me to do now?"

I learned how to do just about everything there was to do on a farm, and I loved it. They raised peanuts, corn, wheat, soybeans, and they had a little tobacco allotment. A man down on the Shiloh farm named Daniel Keel, he would tend to the tobacco. They were mostly row-crop farmers.

They raised a lot of hogs and a lot of Black Angus cows. Josh Satterthwaite taught me just about everything there was to know about a Black Angus cow and how to raise hogs the old-fashioned way, not in these hog factories like they have now. Back then, you would have your whole farm fenced in—Shiloh was fenced in—and you raised hogs in a farrowing house. We had one that would hold 12 sows, and as soon as she had her pigs weaned, we had her out and twelve more would come in and you'd be surprised how many hogs you could raise like that. After the crop was in, we'd turn all the hogs out, all the cows out of the pasture, and they'd glean. You couldn't find a peanut nor a grain of corn nor a soybean out there anywhere. That was the way to make money. That, and being able to do the work yourself. I loved it. I wouldn't take anything in the world for my association with the Satterthwaite family. Especially Josh, his mother Miss Lil, and his daddy, Mr. Jim.

I raised tobacco over in Nash County. My father-in-law lived in Nashville, North Carolina. He was from Taylor's Store, which is 13 miles north of Nashville. When I first knew him, all that land up and down a great area up there was owned by a Taylor or somebody married to one. He ran a filling station and a repair shop in Nashville, but his great love was farming. I had learned to farm from the Satterthwaites. My last year at Chapel Hill, I'd be able to get off Thursday afternoons. I'd come home and spend the night over there at my wife's home and I'd get up the next morning and ask Mr. Taylor, "What would you like me to do today?"

Well, one day, he said, "I want you to go up there on that Billy Mitchell farm"—he rented a lot of land also—"and break up that big field where we're going to plant one crop of tobacco."

I said, "All right." So I hitched up the tractor to a four-bottom plow and went over there to the Billy Mitchell farm and proceeded to break the land like they do in Edgecombe County. People would go into the very center of a field and get the longest rectangle they could make, and then they'd just plow out a rectangle anywhere from 20-25 yards wide and up to 100 yards long, and then they'd start going around in circles to plow out. This keeps your field level and prevents holes in the middle, which gather water, make hard places.

This field was almost a hill because it had been plowed probably for two centuries, going back to when they plowed it with oxen, and it was plowed from the outside in. That made a hill in the middle of it. Well, up in that part of Nash County it's kinda hilly anyhow, but I was taught that a flat field is the best field. And so there I was, about a third of the way into it, and I saw him drive up there in his pickup truck. When he was mad, he'd walk with his forearms sorta parallel to the ground. And he was coming across that field, and I knew he was hot about something. I figured he didn't like the way I was doing it. He was real gruff, and he could cuss. He said, "What in the h—- do you think you're doing?"

I said, "I'm plowing this d—- field, what the h—- do you think I'm doing?"

He said, "That ain't the way to plow a field!"

I said, "It is where I come from!" I said, "What's wrong with this damn field right now is y'all been plowing from the outside for two centuries and made a hill out of it. I'm gonna level it out some."

"How are you going to level it out?"

I said, "If I keep plowing out, it's got to take the dirt to the outside, hadn't it?" He took off his hat and scratched his head, and didn't say another word. He went and got in his pickup and left. That was the worst argument I ever had with him, except one time over a bird dog. This man was a wonderful human being. He was gruff, he was hard, he was a hard worker, but he had a heart of gold. I never spent a minute with him that I didn't enjoy, and that's about the best thing that a Southerner can say about anybody.

He was an excellent bird hunter, and he taught me about it. He was the best damn woods shot I ever saw in my life. I used to tell him, it's because you've got your shotgun sawed off so much and you're so short too, you can shoot around them damn trees! He didn't just love my children, he was enthralled with them. He bought everything that he thought they wanted. And they loved him. I loved him. His name was Percy Errington Taylor. He was from one of the first families of Nash County, North Carolina. They settled in the upper part of Nash County.

The Great Outdoors

The reason Tarboro is here is on account of Tar River. People, when they first settled North Carolina, came up the rivers. Tarboro is the fifth oldest town in North Carolina. By 1730 Tarboro was a right sizable town. It was a port on the Tar River. Fertilizer came up the river on steamboats, and bales of cotton went back down, and cottonseed oil. There was an oil mill up at Shiloh, which is about two and a half miles, maybe three miles by river above town. It burned down in the early part of this century, but there's still part of the old landing there. Tar River was important to me all my life. Being an outdoorsman, and loving the outdoors, just pure-tee loving it . . . if I can't get out there somewhere close to the river for two or three days, I get in a swivet. A swivet is when a southerner can't stand it.

This man Manly Carstarphen was one of my Dutch uncles. He became the forest warden here in Edgecombe County, and I used to spend hours fishing with him down there. Tom Braswell carried me fishing. Cap Wooten ran a barbecue place here for years; Cap used to carry me fishing. I used to go bird hunting with Manly and with Cap, and Tom, and a man here named Porter McNair, and a man that lived right across the street named Harvey McNair. They lived right around the corner from where I lived, up in a new house that was built in 1938, right across the street from what was the high school then. I remember being in a hurry to get out of lab in the fall of the year, 'cause I'd go bird hunting with a doctor that worked over at the med school, who was a friend of Dr. W. Borden Hooks, who was a tremendous friend of my family here in Tarboro.

"Dutch uncles" are a wonderful thing for young boys who love the outdoors, and absorb knowledge from these men like a sponge. The painful part about Dutch uncles occurs when the boy becomes a man and the Dutch uncles become old and leave the boy alone and with thousands of memories that come to his mind almost constantly and an aching heart. When one of them to whom I was particularly close died, I could hear him talking to me for quite a long time.

Another Dutch uncle I had was Mr. Merkle Pulley, who was North Carolina Craftsman of the Year for 1975 and who was a master woodworker. If it could be made out of wood, Merkle could do it. He rebuilt some of the old houses here, reworked them. He's the man responsible for moving the cotton press from where it was, right around the corner on Albemarle Avenue, and completely redoing it.

I saw the last steamboat, the old Tarboro. It was tied up next to the bank down there, just above the mouth of Hendrick's Creek at the old steamboat landing. I knew Mr. Bob Zoeller, who was the engineer on that boat.

When I was about 12 years old, in 1940, my father and mother gave me an Old Town Canoe for Christmas. I've even transported that canoe. I made a little form on a wagon. I could put that canoe on it and hook it behind my bicycle with a piece of rope. I carried it to the river on my wagon. It was called a 14-foot trapper's model, and I still have it. I restored it to its original condition. I have spent in my lifetime thousands and thousands of hours on Tar River by myself in that canoe. Somebody would help me put it in down by what we call the pumping station. I'd paddle upstream as far as I

The Tar River almost reached the bridge when it approached flood stage in 1899 (Courtesy of ECML.)

thought I could go and get back by dark. I used to go up there and spend the night right by myself with a dog I had. I'd sleep under the canoe. You could cock it up. Made a nice little tent, a cozy place to get under there and sleep on a sandbar.

I've killed every game animal in this county except a bear, and I have seen a bear in Edgecombe County in latter years. When they started cutting all the forest down, you'd see a bear come through here every once in awhile. There's been one or two in town. But that boat's held innumerable squirrels, ducks, deer . . . most anything you could eat. And I have gone in that boat from all the way up almost to Enfield—now, that's not all in one trip—but that boat's been all the way from Enfield to the Atlantic Ocean. I didn't cross Pamlico Sound in it. I went across Pamlico Sound on the freight boat run by Van Henry O'Neal, who used to leave Washington every Wednesday night about eleven o'clock going to Ocracoke. Carried that canoe over there and went on the Atlantic Ocean in it.

I killed my first turkey out of that canoe when I was 12 years old, up above Bryant's Bridge, which is the bridge across Fishing Creek between Leggett and Lawrence. Known as Bryant's Bridge, for a black man whose family had owned a piece of land up there, right down on the southern side of the bridge for years. That bridge wasn't the original bridge across Fishing Creek. The original bridge was upstream right in a bend up there, and in real low water, you can still see some of the pilings.

I had numerous boats with outboard engines on them. The first one I ever had, my daddy got a man to build me a boat, and it was so wide you could stand in the middle and you could hardly jump out of it. I had a five-horse Evinrude motor on it, and it would take me all day long to go from the bridge at Tarboro down to Old Sparta and back. The total distance is 16 miles and it would take me from early morning to near 'bout dark to do that. I'm sure that I have spent 50,000 hours of my life on Tar River fishing, hunting, just messing around. There ain't nothing any better for a kid to do to keep him out of trouble than messing around in a boat on Tar River. He ain't going to get up to much devilment down there.

Here's another good story about bees. One spring this very close friend of mine—he was one of my Dutch uncles—named Tom Braswell, who started taking me hunting and fishing with him when I was about seven or eight years old, up until ten days before he died. He was seven feet tall. He was a man possessed of tremendous energy and business sense. He was in the wholesale grocery business and he owned the Shlitz distributorship from Tarboro all the way down to Pea Ridge.

He and I were sitting up the river fishing for rock one day. He called me Little Doc; he called my daddy Big Doc. He talked real slow; he said, "Little Doc?"

I said, "Yeah?"

He said, "See that tree over here?"

I said, "Yeah."

He said, "Look real close. What do you see?"

I said, "I see about a zillion bees!"

He said, "That's a honey tree." That Tom kept beehives. He had a log cabin which was built by his Uncle Fred, on Tar River, right by what we called the red iron bridge, which was a trestle across the river. Tom had a big garden out there, and he had several beehives, and I used to help him sometimes. We'd take honey; I believe it was in August. First time I ever helped him do that I got sick from eating too durn much honey, licking my fingers.

He said, "You just go up there and look in the packhouse and get my bee stuff, get that smoker, get you a pair of those long gloves and that veiled hat, and you get your buddy Fred Hill to go with you and get that crosscut saw and cut that tree down." He said, "I bet there's a durn washtub full of honey in it!"

So, I said, "Fred, we've got to go cut down a honey tree." I said, "We'll saw it down, and then I'll take Tom's smoker and smoke 'em and calm 'em down, and we'll take an ax and bust that thing open and we'll get a washtub full of honey."

We got in my boat and went motoring down there, pulled up to the bank, hauled all that paraphernalia up there, and took that crosscut saw. We made about three or four pulls, and there they came. We dropped the saw, I went flying, jumped off the bank in a running dive and hit the water. I got down in the water and I got a hold of the shaft of the motor and pulled the boat and swam across the river. I stayed in the water. More of them got him; he swam across the river too.

After awhile, they stopped bothering us and we crawled up in the boat. He said, "What're we going to do?"

And I said, "That damn bee stuff can lay there until wintertime, I'm not going near it now!"

I was going to try trapping. I'd always wanted to trap. I think it was 43 years ago. Before I ever even bought the first trap I went to see Osbourne Morris, who was just like an Indian. He had the reputation of being the best trapper that ever was around here. And I asked him if he'd tell me what to do and how. He said, "Well, the main thing you can catch around here is muskrats, but you can catch a coon every once in a while, and you can catch a mink every once in a while. But you're not going to get a big price for the mink, because it doesn't get cold enough in this part of the country, and the people that buy them call them cotton mink, but they bring $14 or $15 a piece." A muskrat was $1.25 and a coon hide was $2.00.

I had a black friend named Dusty Armstrong. Dusty was a woodsman. I asked Dusty if he'd be my skinner.

I went to Shiloh Implement Company one day—that was out on the farm that belonged to the fellow that was like my brother, Josh Sattherwaite—and the Implement Company was owned by his father and J.R., his older brother, a master mechanic. And somebody was saying, "I hear you're going trapping."

I said, "Yeah, now I've got to find a place to go."

There was a man named Nelson Howard, who owned a farm called Cabin Branch Farm on 258 North. He said, "The muskrats are about to ruin my pond. Come out there and trap them."

Tarboro's Main Street, lined with cars after a parade, is pictured in the early 1960s.

I said, "All right."

Well, I had 36 traps, and I cut me some trap stobs. And when you get a trap from the hardware store or order it, you gotta boil them in water with a bunch of walnuts or walnut hulls in there. That takes all the grease off of them and it stains them black, and takes all the scent off. And when you handle them, you need to have a pair of rubber gloves that don't have any scent. So I went out there and set 36 traps. And I saw where a coon had been going. Osbourne had told me, said, "If you see where a big coon has been going, don't put one trap. Put three or four." There was a little inlet-like place off of this pond, small area, and I put four traps in there. I'd go to my traps every other day.

Well, I got up one morning, going out there to Nelson's to check on my traps, and the wind was blowing. I mean blowing hard. I was going around that trap line in a little ol' aluminum boat. The proper name for it would be a pram, because it wasn't but eight feet long. And you'd better be damn particular sitting in it 'cause it would turn over in a heartbeat. It never dumped me over, but I was always scared it would.

I commenced on up, and I was getting pretty close to where that coon set was—when you put out a trap, you call it a set—and I got right up to that little inlet back there, and the wind blew me right in. And there was a damn great big coon, I think he had every one of those traps on him, and he was standing up shaking them and he was madder than hell. And that boat got right up there to him, and that damn coon started coming right over the side of that boat. I took the paddle and whopped him out. He came right back, and I whopped him again. Tried to push so I could get in a position to get the rifle and shoot him. He was fighting mad. We did two or three rounds of him trying to get in the boat with me, until finally I got out of the way of him enough and got the rifle and shot him.

Well, by the time I dispatched that coon, my heart rate had gone up to about 200. I thought for sure he was going to get in that boat with me, and a coon can whup the hell out of you. I tell you, he's a tough customer in close places.

The outdoors—I love it so much that ever since last August I'm trying to write a book about it. I'm writing about the four seasons of the year.

That's about all the stories I've got for today.